Travels In The Interior Of Africa

Vol. II.

by

Mungo Park

Travels In The Interior Of Africa
Vol. II.
by Mungo Park

ISBN: 978-93-57489-49-2

Published by

DOUBLE 9 BOOKS

2/13-B, Ansari Road
Daryaganj, New Delhi – 110002
info@double9books.com
www.double9books.com
Tel. 011-40042856

ABOUT THE AUTHOR

Mungo Park was a Scottish explorer of West Africa. He was born in 1771 and died in 1806. After exploring the upper Niger River in 1796, he wrote a popular and influential travel book called Travels in the Interior Districts of Africa. In it, he thought that the Niger and Congo rivers merged to become the same river, but it was later shown that they are different rivers. Mungo Park was born in Selkirkshire, Scotland, at Foulshiels on the Yarrow Water, close to Selkirk, on a tenant farm that his father rented from the Duke of Buccleuch. Before he went to Selkirk grammar school, he learned at home. At age 14, he went to work for Thomas Anderson, a doctor in Selkirk, as an apprentice. During his apprenticeship, Park became friends with Anderson's son Alexander and met his future wife, Anderson's daughter Allison. Moby-Dick, which was written by Herman Melville in 1851, talks about Mungo Park. In Water Music, written by T. C. Boyle in 1981, Mungo Park is one of the two main characters. In his song "Monsters You Made," which is on the 2020 album Twice as Tall, Burna Boy talks about Park.

CONTENTS

INTRODUCTION.

The first of the two volumes which contain Mungo Park's "Travels in the Interior of Africa" brought him through many perils to the first sight of the Niger, and left him sick and solitary, stripped of nearly all that he possessed, a half-starved white man on a half-starved horse. He was helped on by a bag of cowries from a kindly chief; but in this volume he has not advanced far before he is stripped of all.

There is not in the range of English literature a more interesting traveller's tale than was given to the world in this book which this volume completes. It took the deeper hold upon its readers, because it appeared at a time when English hearts began to be stirred by the wrongs of slavery. But at any time there would be strong human interest in the unconscious painting of the writer's character, as he makes his way over far regions in which no white man had before been seen, with firm resolve and with good temper as well as courage and prudence, which bring him safe through many a hair-breadth escape. There was a true kindness in Mungo Park that found answering kindness and brought out the spirit of humanity in those upon whose goodwill his life depends; in the negroes often, although never in the Moors. There was no flinching in the man, who, when robbed of his horse, stripped to the shirt in a forest and left upon a lion's track, looked down with a botanist's eye on the beauty of a tiny moss at his feet, drew comfort from it, and laboured on with quiet faith in God. The same eye was as quick to recognise the diverse characters of men. In Mungo Park shrewd humour and right feeling went together. Whatever he had to say he said clearly and simply; and it went straight home. He had the good fortune to be born before "picturesque writing" was invented. When we return to the Gambia with Mungo Park under the same escort with a coffle of slaves on their way to be shipped for the use of Christians, from the strength of his unlaboured narrative we get clear knowledge unclouded by a rainbow mist of words. He is of one blood with the sailors in whom Hakluyt delighted.

CHAPTER XVI.
VILLAGES ON THE NIGER—DETERMINES TO GO NO FARTHER EASTWARD.

Being, in the manner that has been related, compelled to leave Sego, I was conducted the same evening to a village about seven miles to the eastward, with some of the inhabitants of which my guide was acquainted, and by whom we were well received. [7] He was very friendly and communicative, and spoke highly of the hospitality of his countrymen, but withal told me that if Jenné was the place of my destination, which he seemed to have hitherto doubted, I had undertaken an enterprise of greater danger than probably I was apprised of; for, although the town of Jenné was nominally a part of the king of Bambarra's dominions, it was in fact, he said, a city of the Moors—the leading part of the inhabitants being bushreens, and even the governor himself, though appointed by Mansong, of the same sect. Thus was I in danger of falling a second time into the hands of men who would consider it not only justifiable, but meritorious, to destroy me, and this reflection was aggravated by the circumstance that the danger increased as I advanced in my journey, for I learned that the places beyond Jenné were under the Moorish influence in a still greater degree than Jenné itself, and Timbuctoo, the great object of my search, altogether in possession of that savage and merciless people, who allow no Christian to live there. But I had now advanced too far to think of returning to the westward on such vague and uncertain information, and determined to proceed; and being accompanied by the guide, I departed from the village on the morning of the 24th. About eight o'clock we passed a large town called Kabba, situated in the midst of a beautiful and highly cultivated country, bearing a greater resemblance to the centre of England than to what I should have supposed had been the middle of Africa. The people were everywhere employed in collecting the fruit of shea trees, from which they prepare the vegetable butter mentioned in former parts of this work. These trees grow in great abundance all over this part of Bambarra. They are not planted by the natives, but are found growing naturally in the woods; and in clearing woodland for cultivation every tree is cut down but the shea. The tree itself very much resembles the American oak, and the fruit—from the kernel of which, being first dried in the sun, the butter is prepared by boiling the kernel in water—has somewhat the appearance of a Spanish olive. The kernel is enveloped in a sweet pulp, under a thin green rind; and the butter produced from it, besides the advantage of its keeping the whole year without salt, is whiter, firmer, and, to my palate, of a richer flavour, than the best butter I ever tasted made from cow's milk. The growth and preparation of this commodity seem to be among the first objects of African industry in this and the neighbouring states, and it constitutes a main article of their inland commerce.

We passed, in the course of the day, a great many villages inhabited chiefly by fishermen, and in the evening about five o'clock arrived at Sansanding, a very large town, containing, as I was told, from eight to ten thousand inhabitants. This place is much resorted to by the Moors, who bring salt from Berroo, and beads and coral from the Mediterranean, to exchange here for gold dust and cotton cloth. This cloth they sell to great advantage in Berroo, and other Moorish countries, where, on account of the want of rain, no cotton is cultivated.

I desired my guide to conduct me to the house in which we were to lodge by the most private way possible. We accordingly rode along between the town and the river, passing by a creek or harbour, in which I observed twenty large canoes, most of them fully loaded, and covered with mats to prevent the rain from injuring the goods. As we proceeded, three other canoes arrived, two with passengers and one with goods. I was happy to find that all the negro inhabitants took me for a Moor, under which character I should probably have passed unmolested, had not a Moor, who was sitting by the river-side, discovered the mistake, and, setting up a loud exclamation, brought together a number of his countrymen.

When I arrived at the house of Counti Mamadi, the dooty of the town, I was surrounded with hundreds of people speaking a variety of different dialects, all equally unintelligible to me. At length, by the assistance of my guide, who acted as interpreter, I understood that one of the spectators pretended to have seen me at one place, and another at some other place; and a Moorish woman absolutely swore that she had kept my house three years at Gallam, on the river Senegal. It was plain that they mistook me for some other person, and I desired two of the most confident to point towards the place where they had seen me. They pointed due south; hence I think it probable that they came from Cape Coast, where they might have seen many white men. Their language was different from any I had yet heard. The Moors now assembled in great number, with their usual arrogance, compelling the negroes to stand at a distance. They immediately began to question me concerning my religion, but finding that I was not master of Arabic, they sent for two men, whom they call *Ilhuidi* (Jews), in hopes that they might be able to converse with me. These Jews, in dress and appearance, very much resemble the Arabs; but though they so far conform to the religion of Mohammed as to recite in public prayers from the Koran, they are but little respected by the negroes; and even the Moors themselves allowed that, though I was a Christian, I was a better man than a Jew. They however insisted that, like the Jews, I must conform so far as to repeat the Mohammedan prayers; and when I attempted to waive the subject by telling them that I could not speak Arabic, one of them, a shereef from Tuat, in the Great Desert, started up and swore by the Prophet that if I refused to go to the mosque, he would be one that would assist in carrying me thither; and there is no doubt that this threat would have been immediately executed had not my landlord interposed on my behalf. He told them that I was the king's stranger, and he could not see me ill-treated whilst I was under his protection. He therefore advised them to let me alone for the night, assuring them that in the morning I should be sent about my business. This somewhat appeased their clamour, but they compelled me to ascend a high seat by the door of the mosque, in order that everybody might see me, for the people had assembled in such numbers as to be quite ungovernable, climbing upon the houses, and squeezing each other, like the spectators at an execution. Upon this seat I remained until sunset, when I was conducted into a neat little hut, with a small court before it, the door of which Counti Mamadi shut, to prevent any person from disturbing me. But this precaution could not exclude the Moors. They climbed over the top of the mud wall, and came in crowds into the court, "in order," they said, "to see me *perform my evening devotions, and eat eggs.*" The former of these ceremonies I did not think proper to comply with, but I told them I had no objection to eat eggs, provided they would bring me eggs to eat. My landlord immediately brought me seven hen's eggs, and was much surprised to find that I could not eat them raw; for it seems to be a prevalent opinion among the inhabitants of the interior that Europeans subsist almost entirely on this diet. When I had succeeded in persuading my landlord that this opinion was without foundation, and that I would gladly partake of any victuals which he might think proper to send me, he ordered a sheep to be killed, and part of it to be dressed for my supper. About midnight, when the Moors had left me, he paid me a visit, and with much earnestness desired me to write him a saphie. "If a Moor's saphie is good," said this hospitable old man, "a white man's must needs be better." I readily furnished him with one, possessed of all the virtues I could concentrate, for it contained the Lord's Prayer. The pen with which it was written was made of a reed; a little charcoal and gum-water made very tolerable ink, and a thin board answered the purpose of paper.

July 25.—Early in the morning, before the Moors were assembled, I departed from Sansanding, and slept the ensuing night at a small town called Sibili, from whence on the day following I reached Nyara, a large town at some distance from the river, where I halted the 27th, to have my clothes washed, and recruit my horse. The dooty there has a very commodious house, flat-roofed, and two storeys high. He showed me some gunpowder of his own manufacturing; and pointed out, as a great curiosity, a little brown monkey that was tied to a stake by the door, telling me that it came from a far distant country called Kong.

July 28.—I departed from Nyara, and reached Nyamee about noon. This town is inhabited chiefly by Foulahs from the kingdom of Masina. The dooty, I know not why, would not receive me, but civilly sent his son on horseback to conduct me to Modiboo, which he assured me was at no great distance.

We rode nearly in a direct line through the woods, but in general went forwards with great circumspection. I observed that my guide frequently stopped and looked under the bushes. On inquiring the reason of this caution he told me that lions were very numerous in that part of the country, and frequently attacked people travelling through the woods. While he was speaking, my horse started, and looking round, I observed a large animal of the camelopard kind standing at a little distance. The neck and fore-legs were very long; the head was furnished with two short black horns, turning backwards; the tail, which reached down to the ham joint, had a tuft of hair at the end. The animal was of a mouse colour, and it trotted away from us in a very sluggish manner—moving its head from side to side, to see if we were pursuing it. Shortly after this, as we were crossing a large open plain, where there were a few scattered bushes, my guide, who was a little way before me, wheeled his horse round in a moment, calling out something in the Foulah language which I did not understand. I inquired in Mandingo what he meant; "*Wara billi billi!*" ("A very large lion!") said he, and made signs for me to ride away. But my horse was too much fatigued; so we rode slowly past the bush from which the animal had given us the alarm. Not seeing anything myself, however, I thought my guide had been mistaken, when the Foulah suddenly put his hand to his mouth, exclaiming, "*Soubah an allahi!*" ("God preserve us!") and, to my great surprise, I then perceived a large red lion, at a short distance from the bush, with his head couched between his forepaws. I expected he would instantly spring upon me, and instinctively pulled my feet from my stirrups to throw myself on the ground, that my horse might become the victim rather than myself. But it is probable the lion was not hungry;

for he quietly suffered us to pass, though we were fairly within his reach. My eyes were so riveted upon this sovereign of the beasts that I found it impossible to remove them until we were at a considerable distance. We now took a circuitous route through some swampy ground, to avoid any more of these disagreeable encounters. At sunset we arrived at Modiboo—a delightful village on the banks of the Niger, commanding a view of the river for many miles both to the east and west. The small green islands (the peaceful retreat of some industrious Foulahs, whose cattle are here secure from the depredations of wild beasts) and the majestic breadth of the river, which is here much larger than at Sego, render the situation one of the most enchanting in the world. Here are caught great plenty of fish, by means of long cotton nets, which the natives make themselves, and use nearly in the same manner as nets are used in Europe. I observed the head of a crocodile lying upon one of the houses, which they told me had been killed by the shepherds in a swamp near the town. These animals are not uncommon in the Niger, but I believe they are not oftentimes found dangerous. They are of little account to the traveller when compared with the amazing swarms of mosquitoes, which rise from the swamps and creeks in such numbers as to harass even the most torpid of the natives; and as my clothes were now almost worn to rags, I was but ill prepared to resist their attacks. I usually passed the night without shutting my eyes, walking backwards and forwards, fanning myself with my hat; their stings raised numerous blisters on my legs and arms, which, together with the want of rest, made me very feverish and uneasy.

July 29.—Early in the morning, my landlord, observing that I was sickly, hurried me away, sending a servant with me as a guide to Kea. But though I was little able to walk, my horse was still less able to carry me; and about six miles to the east of Modiboo, in crossing some rough clayey ground, he fell, and the united strength of the guide and myself could not place him again upon his legs. I sat down for some time beside this worn-out associate of my adventures, but finding him still unable to rise, I took off the saddle and bridle, and placed a quantity of grass before him. I surveyed the poor animal, as he lay panting on the ground, with sympathetic emotion, for I could not suppress the sad apprehension that I should myself, in a short time, lie down and perish in the same manner, of fatigue and hunger. With this foreboding I left my poor horse, and with great reluctance followed my guide on foot along the bank of the river until about noon, when we reached Kea, which I found to be nothing more than a small fishing village. The dooty, a surly old man, who was sitting by the gate, received me very coolly; and when I informed him of my situation, and begged his protection, told me with great indifference that he paid very little attention to fine speeches, and that I should not enter his house. My guide remonstrated in my favour, but to no purpose, for the dooty remained inflexible in his determination. I knew not where to rest my wearied limbs, but was happily relieved by a fishing canoe belonging to Silla, which was at that moment coming down the river. The dooty waved to the fisherman to come near, and desired him to take charge of me as far as Moorzan. The fisherman, after some hesitation, consented to carry me, and I embarked in the canoe in company with the fisherman, his wife, and a boy. The negro who had conducted me from Modiboo now left me. I requested him to look to my horse on his return, and take care of him if he was still alive, which he promised to do.

Departing from Kea, we proceeded about a mile down the river, when the fisherman paddled the canoe to the bank and desired me to jump out. Having tied the canoe to a stake, he stripped off his clothes, and dived for such a length of time that I thought he had actually drowned himself, and was surprised to see his wife behave with so much indifference upon the occasion; but my fears were over when he raised up his head astern of the canoe and called for a rope. With this rope he dived a second time, and then got into the canoe and ordered the boy to assist him in pulling. At length they brought up a large basket, about ten feet in diameter, containing two fine fish, which the fisherman—after returning the basket into the water—immediately carried ashore and hid in the grass. We then went a little farther down and took up another basket, in which was one fish. The fisherman now left us to carry his prizes to some neighbouring market, and the woman and boy proceeded with me in the canoe down the river.

About four o'clock we arrived at Moorzan, a fishing town on the northern bank, from whence I was conveyed across the river to Silla, a large town, where I remained until it was quite dark, under a tree, surrounded by hundreds of people.

With a great deal of entreaty the dooty allowed me to come into his baloon to avoid the rain, but the place was very damp, and I had a smart paroxysm of fever during the night. Worn down by sickness, exhausted with hunger and fatigue, half-naked, and without any article of value by which I might procure provisions, clothes, or lodging, I began to reflect seriously on my situation. I was now convinced, by painful experience, that the obstacles to my farther progress were insurmountable. The tropical rains were already set in with all their violence—the rice grounds and swamps were everywhere overflowed—and in a few days more, travelling of every kind, unless by water, would be completely obstructed. The kowries which remained of the king of Bambarra's present were not sufficient to enable me to hire a canoe for any great distance, and I had but little hopes of subsisting by charity in a country where the Moors have such influence. But, above all, I perceived that

I was advancing more and more within the power of those merciless fanatics, and, from my reception both at Sego and Sansanding, I was apprehensive that, in attempting to reach even Jenné (unless under the protection of some man of consequence amongst them, which I had no means of obtaining), I should sacrifice my life to no purpose, for my discoveries would perish with me. The prospect either way was gloomy. In returning to the Gambia, a journey on foot of many hundred miles presented itself to my contemplation, through regions and countries unknown. Nevertheless, this seemed to be the only alternative, for I saw inevitable destruction in attempting to proceed to the eastward. With this conviction on my mind I hope my readers will acknowledge that I did right in going no farther.

Having thus brought my mind, after much doubt and perplexity, to a determination to return westward, I thought it incumbent on me, before I left Silla, to collect from the Moorish and negro traders all the information I could concerning the farther course of the Niger eastward, and the situation and extent of the kingdoms in its vicinage; and the following few notices I received from such various quarters as induce me to think they are authentic:—

Two short days' journey to the eastward of Silla is the town of Jenné, which is situated on a small island in the river, and is said to contain a greater number of inhabitants than Sego itself, or any other town in Bambarra. At the distance of two days more, the river spreads into a considerable lake, called Dibbie (or the Dark Lake), concerning the extent of which all the information I could obtain was that in crossing it from west to east the canoes lose sight of land one whole day. From this lake the water issues in many different streams, which terminate in two large branches, one whereof flows towards the north-east, and the other to the east; but these branches join at Kabra, which is one day's journey to the southward of Timbuctoo, and is the port or shipping-place of that city. The tract of land which the two streams encircle is called Jinbala, and is inhabited by negroes; and the whole distance by land from Jenné to Timbuctoo is twelve days' journey.

From Kabra, at the distance of eleven days' journey down the stream, the river passes to the southward of Houssa, which is two days' journey distant from the river. Of the farther progress of this great river, and its final exit, all the natives with whom I conversed seemed to be entirely ignorant. Their commercial pursuits seldom induce them to travel farther than the cities of Timbuctoo and Houssa, and as the sole object of those journeys is the acquirement of wealth, they pay little attention to the course of rivers or the geography of countries. It is, however, highly probable that the Niger affords a safe and easy communication between very remote nations. All my informants agreed that many of the negro merchants who arrive at Timbuctoo and Houssa from the eastward speak a different language from that of Bambarra, or any other kingdom with which they are acquainted But even these merchants, it would seem, are ignorant of the termination of the river, for such of them as can speak Arabic describe the amazing length of its course in very general terms, saying only that they believe it runs *to the world's end.*

The names of many kingdoms to the eastward of Houssa are familiar to the inhabitants of Bambarra. I was shown quivers and arrows of very curious workmanship, which I was informed came from the kingdom of Kassina.

On the northern bank of the Niger, at a short distance from Silla, is the kingdom of Masina, which is inhabited by Foulahs. They employ themselves there, as in other places, chiefly in pasturage, and pay an annual tribute to the king of Bambarra for the lands which they occupy.

To the north-east of Masina is situated the kingdom of Timbuctoo, the great object of European research—the capital of this kingdom being one of the principal marts for that extensive commerce which the Moors carry on with the negroes. The hopes of acquiring wealth in this pursuit, and zeal for propagating their religion, have filled this extensive city with Moors and Mohammedan converts. The king himself and all the chief officers of state are Moors; and they are said to be more severe and intolerant in their principles than any other of the Moorish tribes in this part of Africa. I was informed by a venerable old negro, that when he first visited Timbuctoo, he took up his lodging at a sort of public inn, the landlord of which, when he conducted him into his hut, spread a mat on the floor, and laid a rope upon it, saying, "If you are a Mussulman, you are my friend—sit down; but if you are a kafir, you are my slave, and with this rope I will lead you to market." The present king of Timbuctoo is named Abu Abrahima. He is reported to possess immense riches. His wives and concubines are said to be clothed in silk, and the chief officers of state live in considerable splendour. The whole expense of his government is defrayed, as I was told, by a tax upon merchandise, which is collected at the gates of the city.

The city of Houssa (the capital of a large kingdom of the same name, situated to the eastward of Timbuctoo), is another great mart for Moorish commerce. I conversed with many merchants who had visited that city, and they all agreed that it is larger—and more populous than Timbuctoo. The trade, police, and government are nearly the same in both; but in Houssa the negroes are in greater proportion to the Moors, and have some share in the government.

Concerning the small kingdom of Jinbala I was not able to collect much information. The soil is said to be remarkably fertile, and the whole country so full of creeks and swamps that the Moors have hitherto been baffled in every attempt to subdue it. The inhabitants are negroes, and some of them are said to live in considerable affluence, particularly those near the capital, which is a resting-place for such merchants as transport goods from Timbuctoo to the western parts of Africa.

To the southward of Jinbala is situated the negro kingdom of Gotto, which is said to be of great extent. It was formerly divided into a number of petty states, which were governed by their own chiefs; but their private quarrels invited invasion from the neighbouring kingdoms. At length a politic chief of the name of Moossee had address enough to make them unite in hostilities against Bambarra; and on this occasion he was unanimously chosen general—the different chiefs consenting for a time to act under his command. Moossee immediately despatched a fleet of canoes, loaded with provisions, from the banks of the lake Dibbie up the Niger towards Jenné, and with the whole of his army pushed forwards into Bambarra. He arrived on the bank of the Niger opposite to Jenné before the townspeople had the smallest intimation of his approach. His fleet of canoes joined him the same day, and having landed the provisions, he embarked part of his army, and in the night took Jenné by storm. This event so terrified the king of Bambarra that he sent messengers to sue for peace; and in order to obtain it consented to deliver to Moossee a certain number of slaves every year, and return everything that had been taken from the inhabitants of Gotto. Moossee, thus triumphant, returned to Gotto, where he was declared king, and the capital of the country is called by his name.

On the west of Gotto is the kingdom of Baedoo, which was conquered by the present king of Bambarra about seven years ago, and has continued tributary to him ever since.

West of Baedoo is Maniana, the inhabitants of which, according to the best information I was able to collect, are cruel and ferocious—carrying their resentment towards their enemies so far as never to give quarter, and even to indulge themselves with unnatural and disgusting banquets of human flesh.

CHAPTER XVII.
MOORZAN TO TAFFARA.

Having, for the reasons assigned in the last chapter, determined to proceed no farther eastward than Silla, I acquainted the dooty with my intention of returning to Sego, proposing to travel along the southern side of the river; but he informed me that, from the number of creeks and swamps on that side, it was impossible to travel by any other route than along the northern bank, and even that route, he said, would soon be impassable on account of the overflowing of the river. However, as he commended my determination to return westward, he agreed to speak to some one of the fishermen to carry me over to Moorzan. I accordingly stepped into a canoe about eight o'clock in the morning of July 30th, and in about an hour was landed at Moorzan. At this place I hired a canoe for sixty kowries, and in the afternoon arrived at Kea, where, for forty kowries more, the dooty permitted me to sleep in the same hut with one of his slaves. This poor negro, perceiving that I was sickly, and that my clothes were very ragged, humanely lent me a large cloth to cover me for the night.

July 31.—The dooty's brother being going to Modiboo, I embraced the opportunity of accompanying him thither, there being no beaten road. He promised to carry my saddle, which I had left at Kea, when my horse fell down in the woods, as I now proposed to present it to the king of Bambarra.

We departed from Kea at eight o'clock, and about a mile to the westward observed on the bank of the river a great number of earthen jars piled up together. They were very neatly formed, but not glazed, and were evidently of that sort of pottery which is manufactured at Downie (a town to the west of Timbuctoo), and sold to great advantage in different parts of Bambarra. As we approached towards the jars my companion plucked up a large handful of herbage, and threw it upon them, making signs for me to do the same, which I did. He then, with great seriousness told me that these jars belonged to some supernatural power; that they were found in their present situation about two years ago; and as no person had claimed them, every traveller as he passed them, from respect to the invisible proprietor, threw some grass, or the branch of a tree, upon the heap, to defend the jars from the rain.

Thus conversing, we travelled in the most friendly manner, until unfortunately we perceived the footsteps of a lion, quite fresh in the mud, near the river-side. My companion now proceeded with great circumspection; and at last, coming to some thick underwood, he insisted that I should walk before him. I endeavoured to excuse myself, by alleging that I did not know the road; but he obstinately persisted, and, after a few high words and menacing looks, threw down the saddle and went away. This very much disconcerted me; but as I had given up all hopes of obtaining a horse, I could not think of encumbering myself with the saddle, and, taking off the stirrups and girths, I threw the saddle into the river. The negro no sooner saw me throw the saddle into the water than he came running from among the bushes where he had concealed himself, jumped into the river, and by help of his spear, brought out the saddle and ran away with it. I continued my course along the bank; but as the wood was remarkably thick, and I had reason to believe that a lion was at no great distance, I became much alarmed, and took a long circuit through the bushes to avoid him.

About four in the afternoon I reached Modiboo, where I found my saddle. The guide, who had got there before me, being afraid that I should inform the king of his conduct, had brought the saddle with him in a canoe.

While I was conversing with the dooty, and remonstrating against the guide for having left me in such a situation, I heard a horse neigh in one of the huts; and the dooty inquired with a smile if I knew who was speaking to me. He explained himself by telling me that my horse was still alive, and somewhat recovered from his fatigue; but he insisted that I should take him along with me, adding that he had once kept a Moor's horse for four months, and when the horse had recovered and got into good condition, the Moor returned and claimed it, and refused to give him any reward for his trouble.

August 1.—I departed from Modiboo, driving my horse before me, and in the afternoon reached Nyamee; where I remained three days, during which time it rained without intermission, and with such violence that no person could venture out of doors.

August 5.—I departed from Nyamee; but the country was so deluged that I was frequently in danger of losing the road, and had to wade across the savannas for miles together, knee-deep in water. Even the corn ground, which is the driest land in the country, was so completely flooded that my horse twice stuck fast in the mud, and was not got out without the greatest difficulty.

In the evening of the same day I arrived at Nyara, where I was well received by the dooty; and as the 6th was rainy I did not depart until the morning of the 7th; but the water had swelled to such a height, that in many places the road was scarcely passable, and though I waded breast-deep across the swamps I could only reach a small village called Nemaboo, where however, for a hundred kowries, I procured from some Foulahs plenty of corn for my horse and milk for myself.

August 8.—The difficulties I had experienced the day before made me anxious to engage a fellow-traveller, particularly as I was assured that, in the course of a few days, the country would be so completely overflowed as to render the road utterly impassable; but though I offered two hundred kowries for a guide, nobody would accompany me. However, on the morning following, August 9th, a Moor and his wife, riding upon two bullocks, and bound for Sego with salt, passed the village, and agreed to take me along with them; but I found them of little service, for they were wholly unacquainted with the road, and being accustomed to a sandy soil, were very bad travellers. Instead of wading before the bullocks to feel if the ground was solid, the woman boldly entered the first swamp, riding upon the top of the load; but when she had proceeded about two hundred yards the bullock sunk into a hole, and threw both the load and herself among the reeds. The frightened husband stood for some time seemingly petrified with horror, and suffered his wife to be almost drowned before he went to her assistance.

About sunset we reached Sibity, but the dooty received me very coolly; and when I solicited for a guide to Sansanding he told me his people were otherwise employed. I was shown into a damp old hut, where I passed a very uncomfortable night; for when the walls of the huts are softened by the rain they frequently become too weak to support the weight of the roof. I heard three huts fall during the night, and was apprehensive that the hut I lodged in would be the fourth. In the morning, as I went to pull some grass for my horse, I counted fourteen huts which had fallen in this manner since the commencement of the rainy season.

It continued to rain with great violence all the 10th; and as the dooty refused to give me any provisions, I purchased some corn, which I divided with my horse.

August 11.—The dooty compelled me to depart from the town, and I set out for Sansanding without any great hopes of faring better than I had done at Sibity; for I learned, from people who came to visit me, that a report prevailed, and was universally believed, that I had come to Bambarra as a spy; and as Mansong had not admitted me into his presence, the dooties of the different towns were at liberty to treat me in what manner they pleased.

From repeatedly hearing the same story I had no doubt of the truth of it; but as there was no alternative I determined to proceed, and a little before sunset I arrived at Sansanding. My reception was what I expected. Counti Mamadi, who had been so kind to me formerly, scarcely gave me welcome. Every one wished to shun me; and my landlord sent a person to inform me that a very unfavourable report was received from Sego concerning me, and that he wished me to depart early in the morning. About ten o'clock at night Counti Mamadi himself came privately to me, and informed me that Mansong had despatched a canoe to Jenné to bring me back; and he was afraid I should find great difficulty in going to the west country. He advised me therefore to depart from Sansanding before daybreak, and cautioned me against stopping at Diggani, or any town near Sego.

August 12.—I departed from Sansanding, and reached Kabba in the afternoon. As I approached the town I was surprised to see several people assembled at the gate, one of whom, as I advanced, came running towards me, and taking my horse by the bridle, led me round the walls of the town, and then, pointing to the west, told me to go along, or it would fare worse with me. It was in vain that I represented the danger of being benighted in the woods, exposed to the inclemency of the weather and the fury of wild beasts. "Go along!" was all the answer; and a number of people coming up and urging me in the same manner, with great earnestness, I suspected that some of the king's messengers, who were sent in search of me, were in the town, and that these negroes, from mere kindness, conducted me past it with a view to facilitate my escape. I accordingly took the road for Sego, with the uncomfortable prospect of passing the night on the branches of a tree. After travelling about three miles, I came to a small village near the road. The dooty was splitting sticks by the gate, but I found I could have no admittance, and when I attempted to enter, he jumped up, and with the stick he held in his hand, threatened to strike me off the horse if I presumed to advance another step.

At a little distance from this village (and further from the road) is another small one. I conjectured that, being rather out of the common route, the inhabitants might have fewer objections to give me house-room for the night; and having crossed some cornfields, I sat down under a tree by the well. Two or three women came to draw water, and one of them, perceiving I was a stranger, inquired whither I was going. I told her I was going for Sego, but being benighted on the road, I wished to stay at the village until morning, and begged she would acquaint the dooty with my situation. In a little time the dooty sent for me, and permitted me to sleep in a large baloon.

August 13.—About ten o'clock I reached a small village within half a mile of Sego, where I endeavoured, but in vain, to procure some provisions. Every one seemed anxious to avoid me; and I can plainly perceive, by the looks and behaviour of the inhabitants, that some very unfavourable accounts had been circulated concerning me. I was again informed that Mansong had sent people to apprehend me, and the dooty's son told me I had no time to lose if I wished to get safe out of Bambarra. I now fully saw the danger of my situation, and determined to avoid Sego altogether. I accordingly mounted my horse, and taking the road for Diggani, travelled as fast as I could till I was out of sight of the villagers, when I struck to the westward, through high grass and swampy ground. About noon I stopped under a tree to consider what course to take, for I had now no doubt that the Moors and slatees had misinformed the king respecting the object of my mission, and that people were absolutely in search of me to convey me a prisoner to Sego. Sometimes I had thoughts of swimming my horse across the Niger, and going to the southward for Cape Coast, but reflecting that I had ten days to travel before I should reach Kong, and afterwards an extensive country to traverse, inhabited by various nations with whose language and manners I was totally unacquainted, I relinquished this scheme, and judged that I should better answer the purpose of my mission by proceeding to the westward along the Niger, endeavouring to ascertain how far the river was navigable in that direction. Having resolved upon this course, I proceeded accordingly, and a little before sunset arrived at a Foulah village called Sooboo, where, for two hundred kowries, I procured lodging for the night.

August 14.—I continued my course along the bank of the river, through a populous and well-cultivated country. I passed a walled town called Kamalia [35] without stopping, and at noon rode through a large town called Samee, where there happened to be a market, and a number of people assembled in an open place in the middle of the town, selling cattle, cloth, corn, &c. I rode through the midst of them without being much observed, every one taking me for a Moor. In the afternoon I arrived at a small village called Binni, where I agreed with the dooty's son, for one hundred kowries, to allow me to stay for the night; but when the dooty returned, he insisted that I should instantly leave the place, and if his wife and son had not interceded for me, I must have complied.

August 15.—About nine o'clock I passed a large town called Sai, which very much excited my curiosity. It is completely surrounded by two very deep trenches, at about two hundred yards distant from the walls. On the top of the trenches are a number of square towers, and the whole has the appearance of a regular fortification.

About noon I came to the village of Kaimoo, situated upon the bank of the river, and as the corn I had purchased at Sibili was exhausted, I endeavoured to purchase a fresh supply, but was informed that corn was become very scarce all over the country, and though I offered fifty kowries for a small quantity, no person would sell me any. As I was about to depart, however, one of the villagers (who probably mistook me for some Moorish shereef) brought me some as a present, only desiring me to bestow my blessing upon him, which I did in plain English, and he received it with a thousand acknowledgments. Of this present I made my dinner, and it was the third successive day that I had subsisted entirely upon raw corn.

In the evening I arrived at a small village called Song, the surly inhabitants of which would not receive me, nor so much as permit me to enter the gate; but as lions were very numerous in this neighbourhood, and I had frequently, in the course of the day, observed the impression of their feet on the road, I resolved to stay in the vicinity of the village. Having collected some grass for my horse, I accordingly lay down under a tree by the gate. About ten o'clock I heard the hollow roar of a lion at no great distance, and attempted to open the gate, but the people from within told me that no person must attempt to enter the gate without the dooty's permission. I begged them to inform the dooty that a lion was approaching the village, and I hoped he would allow me to come within the gate. I waited for an answer to this message with great anxiety, for the lion kept prowling round the village, and once advanced so very near me that I heard him rustling among the grass, and climbed the tree for safety. About midnight the dooty, with some of his people, opened the gate, and desired me to come in. They were convinced, they said, that I was not a Moor, for no Moor ever waited any time at the gate of a village without cursing the inhabitants.

August 16.—About ten o'clock I passed a considerable town, with a mosque, called Jabbee. Here the country begins to rise into hills, and I could see the summits of high mountains to the westward. About noon I stopped at a small village near Yamina, where I purchased some corn, and dried my papers and clothes.

The town of Yamina at a distance has a very fine appearance. It covers nearly the same extent of ground as Sansanding, but having been plundered by Daisy, king of Kaarta, about four years ago, it has not yet resumed its former prosperity, nearly one-half of the town being nothing but a heap of ruins. However, it is still a considerable place, and is so much frequented by the Moors that I did not think it safe to lodge in it, but in order to satisfy myself respecting its population and extent, I resolved to ride through it, in doing which I observed a great many Moors sitting upon the bentangs, and other places of public resort. Everybody looked at me with astonishment, but as I rode briskly along they had no time to ask questions.

I arrived in the evening at Farra, a walled village, where, without much difficulty, I procured a lodging for the night.

August 17.—Early in the morning I pursued my journey, and at eight o'clock passed a considerable town called Balaba, after which the road quits the plain, and stretches along the side of the hill. I passed in the course of this day the ruins of three towns, the inhabitants of which were all carried away by Daisy, king of Kaarta, on the same day that he took and plundered Yamina. Near one of these ruins I climbed a tamarind-tree, but found the fruit quite green and sour, and the prospect of the country was by no means inviting, for the high grass and bushes seemed completely to obstruct the road, and the low lands were all so flooded by the river, that the Niger had the appearance of an extensive lake. In the evening I arrived at Kanika, where the dooty, who was sitting upon an elephant's hide at the gate, received me kindly, and gave me for supper some milk and meal, which I considered (as to a person in my situation it really was) a very great luxury.

August 18.—By mistake I took the wrong road, and did not discover my error until I had travelled nearly four miles, when, coming to an eminence, I observed the Niger considerably to the left. Directing my course towards it, I travelled through long grass and bushes with great difficulty until two o'clock in thee afternoon, when I came to a comparatively small but very rapid river, which I took at first for a creek, or one of the streams of the Niger. However, after I had examined it with more attention, I was convinced that it was a distinct river, and as the road evidently crossed it (for I could see the pathway on the opposite side), I sat down upon the bank in hopes that some traveller might arrive who would give me the necessary information concerning the fording-place—for the banks were so covered with reeds and bushes that it would have been almost impossible to land on the other side, except at the pathway, which, on account of the rapidity of the stream, it seemed very difficult to reach. No traveller however arriving, and there being a great appearance of rain, I examined the grass and bushes for some way up the bank, and determined upon entering the river considerably above the pathway, in order to reach the other side before the stream had swept me too far down. With this view I fastened my clothes upon the saddle, and was standing up to the neck in water, pulling my horse by the bridle to make him follow me, where a man came accidentally to the place, and seeing me in the water, called to me with great vehemence to come out. The alligators, he said, would devour both me and my horse, if we attempted to swim over. When I had got out, the stranger, who had never before seen a European, seemed wonderfully surprised. He twice put his hand to his mouth, exclaiming, in a low tone of voice, "God preserve me! who is this?" but when he heard me speak the Bambarra tongue, and found that I was going the same way as himself, he promised to assist me in crossing the river, the name of which he said was Frina. He then went a little way along the bank, and called to some person, who answered from the other side. In a short time a canoe with two boys came paddling from among the reeds. These boys agreed for fifty kowries to transport me and my horse over the river, which was effected without much difficulty, and I arrived in the evening at Taffara, a walled town, and soon discovered that the language of the natives was improved from the corrupted dialect of Bambarra to the pure Mandingo.

CHAPTER XVIII.
DESPAIRING THOUGHTS—ARRIVAL AT SIBIDOOLOO.

On my arrival at Taffara I inquired for the dooty, but was informed that he had died a few days before my arrival, and that there was at that moment a meeting of the chief men for electing another, there being some dispute about the succession. It was probably owing to this unsettled state of the town that I experienced such a want of hospitality in it, for though I informed the inhabitants that I should only remain with them for one night, and assured them that Mansong had given me some kowries to pay for my lodging, yet no person invited me to come in, and I was forced to sit alone under the bentang-tree, exposed to the rain and wind of a tornado, which lasted with great violence until midnight. At this time the stranger who had assisted me in crossing the river paid me a visit, and observing that I had not found a lodging, invited me to take part of his supper, which he had brought to the door of his hut; for, being a guest himself, he could not, without his landlord's consent, invite me to come in. After this I slept upon some wet grass in the corner of a court. My horse fared still worse than myself, the corn I purchased being all expended, and I could not procure a supply.

August 20.—I passed the town of Jaba, and stopped a few minutes at a village called Somino, where I begged and obtained some coarse food, which the natives prepare from the husks of corn, and call *boo*. About two o'clock I came to the village of Sooha, and endeavoured to purchase some corn from the dooty, who was sitting by the gate, but without success. I then requested a little food by way of charity, but was told he had none to spare. Whilst I was examining the countenance of this inhospitable old man, and endeavouring to find out the cause of the sullen discontent which was visible in his eye, he called to a slave who was working in the cornfield at a little distance, and ordered him to bring his hoe along with him. The dooty then told him to dig a hole in the ground, pointing to a spot at no great distance. The slave, with his hoe, began to dig a pit in the earth, and the dooty, who appeared to be a man of very fretful disposition, kept muttering and talking to himself until the pit was almost finished, when he repeatedly pronounced the words *"dankatoo"* ("good for nothing")—"*jankra lemen*" ("a real plague")—which expressions I thought could be applied to nobody but myself; and as the pit had very much the appearance of a grave, I thought it prudent to mount my horse, and was about to decamp, when the slave, who had before gone into the village, to my surprise returned with the corpse of a boy about nine or ten years of age, quite naked. The negro carried the body by a leg and an arm, and threw it into the pit with a savage indifference which I had never before seen. As he covered the body with earth, the dooty often expressed himself, "*naphula attiniata*" ("money lost"), whence I concluded that the boy had been one of his slaves.

Departing from this shocking scene, I travelled by the side of the river until sunset, when I came to Koolikorro, a considerable town, and a great market for salt. Here I took up my lodging at the house of a Bambarran, who had formerly been the slave of a Moor, and in that character had travelled to Aroan, Towdinni, and many other places in the Great Desert; but turning Mussulman, and his master dying at Jenné, he obtained his freedom and settled at this place, where he carries on a considerable trade in salt, cotton cloth, &c. His knowledge of the world had not lessened that superstitious confidence in saphies and charms which he had imbibed in his earlier years, for when he heard that I was a Christian, he immediately thought of procuring a saphie, and for this purpose brought out his *walha*, or writing-board, assuring me that he would dress me a supper of rice if I would write him a saphie to protect him from wicked men. The proposal was of too great consequence to me to be refused. I therefore wrote the board full, from top to bottom, on both sides; and my landlord, to be certain of having the whole force of the charm, washed the writing from the board into a calabash with a little water, and having said a few prayers over it, drank this powerful draught; after which, lest a single word should escape, he licked the board until it was quite dry. A saphie-writer was a man of too great consequence to be long concealed; the important information was carried to the dooty, who sent his son with half a sheet of writing-paper, desiring me to write him a *naphula saphie* (a charm to procure wealth). He brought me, as a present, some meal and milk, and when I had finished the saphie, and read it to him with an audible voice, he seemed highly satisfied with his bargain, and promised to bring me in the morning some milk for my breakfast. When I had finished my supper of rice and salt, I laid myself down upon a bullock's hide, and slept very quietly until morning, this being the first good meal and refreshing sleep that I had enjoyed for a long time.

August 21.—At daybreak I departed from Koolikorro, and about noon passed the villages of Kayoo and Toolumbo. In the afternoon I arrived at Marraboo, a large town, and, like Koolikorro, famous for its trade in salt. I was conducted to the house of a Kaartan, of the tribe of Jower, by whom

I was well received. This man had acquired a considerable property in the slave-trade, and, from his hospitality to strangers, was called, by way of pre-eminence, *jatee* (the landlord), and his house was a sort of public inn for all travellers. Those who had money were well lodged, for they always made him some return for his kindness, but those who had nothing to give were content to accept whatever he thought proper; and as I could not rank myself among the moneyed men, I was happy to take up my lodging in the same but with seven poor fellows who had come from Kancaba in a canoe. But our landlord sent us some victuals.

August 22—One of the landlord's servants went with me a little way from the town to show me what road to take, but, whether from ignorance or design I know not, he directed me wrong, and I did not discover my mistake until the day was far advanced, when, coming to a deep creek, I had some thoughts of turning back, but as by that means I foresaw that I could not possibly reach Bammakoo before night, I resolved to cross it, and, leading my horse close to the brink, I went behind him and pushed him headlong into the water, and then taking the bridle in my teeth, swam over to the other side. About four o'clock in the afternoon, having altered my course from the river towards the mountains, I came to a small pathway which led to a village called Frookaboo, where I slept.

August 23—Early in the morning I set out for Bammakoo, at which place I arrived about five o'clock in the afternoon. I had heard Bammakoo much talked of as a great market for salt, and I felt rather disappointed to find it only a middling town, not quite so large as Marraboo; however, the smallness of its size is more than compensated by the richness of its inhabitants, for when the Moors bring their salt through Kaarta or Bambarra, they constantly rest a few days at this place, and the negro merchants here, who are well acquainted with the value of salt in different kingdoms, frequently purchase by wholesale, and retail it to great advantage. Here I lodged at the house of a Serawoolli negro, and was visited by a number of Moors. They spoke very good Mandingo, and were more civil to me than their countrymen had been. One of them had travelled to Rio Grande, and spoke very highly of the Christians. He sent me in the evening some boiled rice and milk. I now endeavoured to procure information concerning my route to the westward from a slave merchant who had resided some years on the Gambia. He gave me some imperfect account of the distance, and enumerated the names of a great many places that lay in the way, but withal told me that the road was impassable at this season of the year: he was even afraid, he said, that I should find great difficulty in proceeding any farther; as the road crossed the Joliba at a town about half a day's journey to the westward of Bammakoo, and there being no canoes at that place large enough to receive my horse, I could not possibly get him over for some months to come. This was an obstruction of a very serious nature; but as I had no money to maintain myself even for a few days, I resolved to push on, and if I could not convey my horse across the river, to abandon him, and swim over myself. In thoughts of this nature I passed the night, and in the morning consulted with my landlord how I should surmount the present difficulty. He informed me that one road still remained, which was indeed very rocky, and scarcely passable for horses, but that if I had a proper guide over the hills to a town called Sibidooloo, he had no doubt but with patience and caution I might travel forwards through Manding. I immediately applied to the dooty, and was informed that a *jilli kea* (singing man) was about to depart for Sibidooloo, and would show me the road over the hills. With this man, who undertook to be my conductor, I travelled up a rocky glen about two miles, when we came to a small village, and here my musical fellow-traveller found out that he had brought me the wrong road. He told me that the horse-road lay on the other side of the hill, and throwing his drum on his back, mounted up the rocks where, indeed, no horse could follow him, leaving me to admire his agility, and trace out a road for myself. As I found it impossible to proceed, I rode back to the level ground, and directing my course to the eastward, came about noon to another glen, and discovered a path on which I observed the marks of horses' feet. Following this path I came in a short time to some shepherds' huts, where I was informed that I was in the right road, but that I could not possibly reach Sibidooloo before night.

A little before sunset I descended on the north-west side of this ridge of hills, and as I was looking about for a convenient tree under which to pass the night (for I had no hopes of reaching any town) I descended into a delightful valley, and soon afterwards arrived at a romantic village called Kooma. This village is surrounded by a high wall, and is the sole property of a Mandingo merchant, who fled hither with his family during a former war. The adjacent fields yield him plenty of corn, his cattle roam at large in the valley, and the rocky hills secure him from the depredations of war. In this obscure retreat he is seldom visited by strangers, but whenever this happens he makes the weary traveller welcome. I soon found myself surrounded by a circle of the harmless villagers. They asked a thousand questions about my country, and, in return for my information, brought corn and milk for myself, and grass for my horse, kindled a fire in the hut where I was to sleep, and appeared very anxious to serve me.

August 25.—I departed from Kooma, accompanied by two shepherds who were going towards Sibidooloo. The road was very steep and rocky, and as my horse had hurt his feet much in coming from Bammakoo, he travelled slowly and with great difficulty, for in many places the ascent was so sharp, and the declivities so great, that if he had made one false step he must inevitably have been dashed to pieces. The shepherds being anxious to proceed, gave themselves little trouble about me or my horse, and kept walking on at a considerable distance. It was about eleven o'clock, as I stopped to drink a little water at a rivulet (my companions being near a quarter of a mile before me), that I heard some people calling to each other, and presently a loud screaming, as from a person in great distress. I immediately conjectured that a lion had taken one of the shepherds, and mounted my horse to have a better view of what had happened. The noise, however, ceased, and I rode slowly towards the place from whence I thought it had proceeded, calling out, but without receiving any answer. In a little time, however, I perceived one of the shepherds lying among the long grass near the road, and though I could see no blood upon him, I concluded he was dead. But when I came close to him, he whispered to me to stop, telling me that a party of armed men had seized upon his companion, and shot two arrows at himself as he was making his escape. I stopped to consider what course to take, and looking round, saw at a little distance a man sitting upon the stump of a tree. I distinguished also the heads of six or seven more, sitting among the grass, with muskets in their hands. I had now no hopes of escaping, and therefore determined to ride forward towards them. As I approached them, I was in hopes they were elephant-hunters; and by way of opening the conversation inquired if they had shot anything, but without returning an answer one of them ordered me to dismount, and then, as if recollecting himself, waved with his hand for me to proceed. I accordingly rode past, and had with some difficulty crossed a deep rivulet, when I heard somebody holloa, and looking behind, saw those I had taken for elephant-hunters running after me, and calling out to me to turn back. I stopped until they were all come up, when they informed me that the king of the Foulahs had sent them on purpose to bring me, my horse, and everything that belonged to me, to Fooladoo, and that therefore I must turn back and go along with them. Without hesitating a moment, I turned round and followed them, and we travelled together nearly a quarter of a mile without exchanging a word; when, coming to a dark place in a wood, one of them said in the Mandingo language, "This place will do," and immediately snatched my hat from my head. Though I was by no means free of apprehension, yet I resolved to show as few signs of fear as possible, and therefore told them that unless my hat was returned to me I should proceed no farther. But before I had time to receive an answer another drew his knife, and seizing upon a metal button which remained upon my waistcoat, cut it off and put it into his pocket. Their intentions were obvious, and I thought that the easier they were permitted to rob me of everything, the less I had to fear. I therefore allowed them to search my pockets without resistance, and examine every part of my apparel, which they did with the most scrupulous exactness. But observing that I had one waistcoat under another, they insisted that I should cast them both off; and at last, to make sure work, they stripped me quite naked. Even my half-boots (though the sole of one of them was tied on to my foot with a broken bridle rein) were minutely inspected. Whilst they were examining the plunder, I begged them, with great earnestness, to return my pocket-compass; but when I pointed it out to them as it was lying on the ground, one of the banditti, thinking I was about to take it up, cocked his musket, and swore that he would lay me dead upon the spot if I presumed to put my hand upon it. After this, some of them went away with my horse, and the remainder stood considering whether they should leave me quite naked, or allow me something to shelter me from the sun. Humanity at last prevailed; they returned me the worst of the two shirts and a pair of trousers; and, as they went away, one of them threw back my hat, in the crown of which I kept my memorandums, and this was probably the reason they did not wish to keep it. After they were gone, I sat for some time looking round me within amazement and terror. Whichever way I turned, nothing appeared but danger and difficulty. I saw myself in the midst of a vast wilderness, in the depth of the rainy season—naked and alone, surrounded by savage animals, and men still more savage. I was five hundred miles from the nearest European settlement. All these circumstances crowded at once on my recollection, and I confess that my spirits began to fail me. I considered my fate as certain, and that I had no alternative but to lie down and perish. The influence of religion, however, aided and supported me. I reflected that no human prudence or foresight could possibly have averted my present sufferings. I was indeed a stranger in a strange land, yet I was still under the protecting eye of that Providence who has condescended to call Himself the stranger's Friend. At this moment, painful as my reflections were, the extraordinary beauty of a small moss in fructification irresistibly caught my eye. I mention this to show from what trifling circumstances the mind will sometimes derive consolation; for though the whole plant was not larger than the top of one of my fingers, I could not contemplate the delicate conformation of its roots, leaves, and capsula without admiration. Can that Being, thought I, who planted, watered, and brought to perfection, in this obscure part of the world, a thing which appears of so small importance, look within unconcern upon the situation and sufferings of creatures formed after His own image? Surely not! Reflections like these would not allow me to despair. I started up, and, disregarding both hunger and fatigue, travelled forwards, assured that relief was at hand; and I was not disappointed. In a short time I came to a small village, at the entrance of which I overtook the two shepherds who had come with me from Kooma. They were much surprised to see me; for they said they never doubted that the Foulahs, when they had robbed, had murdered me. Departing from this village, we travelled over several rocky ridges, and at sunset arrived at Sibidooloo, the frontier town of the kingdom of Manding.

CHAPTER XIX.
ILLNESS AT KAMALIA AND KINDNESS OF THE NATIVES.

The town of Sibidooloo is situated in a fertile valley, surrounded with high, rocky hills. It is scarcely accessible for horses, and during the frequent wars between the Bambarrans, Foulahs, and Mandingoes has never once been plundered by an enemy. When I entered the town, the people gathered round me and followed me into the baloon, where I was presented to the dooty or chief man, who is here called mansa, which usually signifies king. Nevertheless, it appeared to me that the government of Manding was a sort of republic, or rather an oligarchy—every town having a particular mansa, and the chief power of the state, in the last resort, being lodged in the assembly of the whole body. I related to the mansa the circumstances of my having been robbed of my horse and apparel; and my story was confirmed by the two shepherds. He continued smoking his pipe all the time I was speaking; but I had no sooner finished, than, taking his pipe from his mouth, and tossing up the sleeve of his cloak with an indignant air—"Sit down," said he; "you shall have everything restored to you; I have sworn it:"—and then turning to an attendant, "Give the white man," said he, "a draught of water; and with the first light of the morning go over the hills, and inform the dooty of Bammakoo that a poor white man, the king of Bambarra's stranger, has been robbed by the king of Fooladoo's people."

I little expected, in my forlorn condition, to meet with a man who could thus feel for my sufferings. I heartily thanked the mansa for his kindness, and accepted his invitation to remain with him until the return of the messenger. I was conducted into a hut and had some victuals sent me, but the crowd of people which assembled to see me—all of whom commiserated my misfortunes, and vented imprecations against the Foulahs—prevented me from sleeping until past midnight. Two days I remained without hearing any intelligence of my horse or clothes; and as there was at this time a great scarcity of provisions, approaching even to famine, all over this part of the country, I was unwilling to trespass any farther on the mansa's generosity, and begged permission to depart to the next village. Finding me very anxious to proceed, he told me that I might go as far as a town called Wonda, where he hoped I would remain a few days until I heard some account of my horse, etc.

I departed accordingly on the next morning, the 28th, and stopped at some small villages for refreshment. I was presented at one of them with a dish which I had never before seen. It was composed of the blossoms or *antheræ* of the maize, stewed in milk and water. It is eaten only in time of great scarcity. On the 30th, about noon, I arrived at Wonda, a small town with a mosque, and surrounded by a high wall. The mansa, who was a Mohammedan, acted in two capacities—as chief magistrate of the town, and schoolmaster to the children. He kept his school in an open shed, where I was desired to take up my lodging until some account should arrive from Sibidooloo concerning my horse and clothes; for though the horse was of little use to me, yet the few clothes were essential, The little raiment upon me could neither protect me from the sun by day, nor the dews and mosquitoes by night: indeed, my shirt was not only worn thin like a piece of muslin, but withal so very dirty that I was happy to embrace an opportunity of washing it, which having done, and spread it upon a bush, I sat down naked in the shade until it was dry.

Ever since the commencement of the rainy season my health had been greatly on the decline. I had often been affected with slight paroxysms of fever; and from the time of leaving Bammakoo the symptoms had considerably increased. As I was sitting in the manner described, the fever returned with such violence that it very much alarmed me; the more so as I had no medicine to stop its progress, nor any hope of obtaining that care and attention which my situation required.

I remained at Wonda nine days, during which time I experienced the regular return of the fever every day. And though I endeavoured as much as possible to conceal my distress from my landlord, and frequently lay down the whole day out of his sight, in a field of corn—conscious how burdensome I was to him and his family in a time of such great scarcity—yet I found that he was apprised of my situation; and one morning, as I feigned to be asleep by the fire, he observed to his wife that they were likely to find me a very troublesome and chargeable guest; for that, in my present sickly state, they should be obliged, for the sake of their good name, to maintain me until I recovered or died.

The scarcity of provisions was certainly felt at this time most severely by the poor people, as the following circumstance most painfully convinced me:—Every evening during my stay I observed five or six women come to the mansa's house, and receive each of them a certain quantity of corn. As I knew how valuable this article was at this juncture, I inquired of the mansa whether he maintained these poor women from pure bounty, or expected a return when the harvest should be gathered in. "Observe that boy," said he (pointing to a fine child about five years of age); "his mother has sold him to me for forty days' provision for herself and the rest of her family. I have bought another boy in the same manner." Good God! thought I, what must a mother suffer before she sells her own child! I could not get this melancholy subject out of my mind; and the next night, when the women returned for their allowance, I desired the boy to point out to me his mother, which he did. She was much emaciated, but had nothing cruel or savage in her countenance; and when she had received her corn, she came and talked to her son with as much cheerfulness as if he had still been under her care.

September 6.—Two people arrived from Sibidooloo, bringing with them my horse and clothes; but I found that my pocket-compass was broken to pieces. This was a great loss, which I could not repair.

September 7.—As my horse was grazing near the brink of a well the ground gave way and he fell in. The well was about ten feet in diameter, and so very deep that when I saw my horse snorting in the water I thought it was impossible to save him. The inhabitants of the village, however, immediately assembled, and having tied together a number of withes, [58] they lowered a man down into the well, who fastened those withes round the body of the horse; and the people, having first drawn up the man, took hold of the withes and, to my surprise, pulled the horse out with the greatest facility. The poor animal was now reduced to a mere skeleton, and the roads were scarcely passable, being either very rocky, or else full of mud and water. I therefore found it impracticable to travel with him any farther, and was happy to leave him in the hands of one who, I thought, would take care of him. I accordingly presented him to my landlord, and desired him to send my saddle and bridle as a present to the mansa of Sibidooloo, being the only return I could make him for having taken so much trouble in procuring my horse and clothes.

I now thought it necessary, sick as I was, to take leave of my hospitable landlord. On the morning of September 8th, when I was about to depart, he presented me with his spear, as a token of remembrance, and a leather bag to contain my clothes. Having converted my half-boots into sandals, I travelled with more ease, and slept that night at a village called Ballanti. On the 9th I reached Nemacoo; but the mansa of the village thought fit to make me sup upon the chameleon's dish. By way of apology, however, he assured me the next morning that the scarcity of corn was such that he could not possibly allow me any. I could not accuse him of unkindness, as all the people actually appeared to be starving.

September 10.—It rained hard all day, and the people kept themselves in their huts. In the afternoon I was visited by a negro, named Modi Lemina Taura, a great trader, who, suspecting my distress, brought me some victuals, and promised to conduct me to his own house at Kinyeto the day following.

September 11.—I departed from Nemacoo, and arrived at Kinyeto in the evening; but having hurt my ankle in the way, it swelled and inflamed so much that I could neither walk nor set my foot to the ground the next day without great pain. My landlord, observing this, kindly invited me to stop with him a few days, and I accordingly remained at his house until the 14th, by which the I felt much relieved, and could walk with the help of a staff. I now set out, thanking my landlord for his great care and attention; and being accompanied by a young man who was travelling the same way, I proceeded for Jerijang, a beautiful and well-cultivated district, the mansa of which is reckoned the most powerful chief of any in Manding.

On the 15th I reached Dosita, a large town, where I stayed one day on account of the rain; but I continued very sickly, and was slightly delirious in the night. On the 17th I set out for Mansia, a considerable town, where small quantities of gold are collected. The road led over a high, rocky hill, and my strength and spirits were so much exhausted that before I could reach the top of the hill I was forced to lie down three times, being very faint and sickly. I reached Mansia in the afternoon. The mansa of this town had the character of being very inhospitable; he, however, sent me a little corn for my supper, but demanded something in return; and when I assured him that I had nothing of value in my possession, he told me (as if in jest) that my white skin should not defend me if I told him lies. He then showed me the hut wherein I was to sleep, but took away my spear, saying that it should be returned to me in the morning. This trifling circumstance, when joined to the character I had heard of the man, made me rather suspicious of him, and I privately desired one of the inhabitants of the place, who had a bow and a quiver, to sleep in the same hunt with me. About midnight I heard somebody approach the door, and, observing the moonlight strike suddenly into the hut, I started up and saw a man stepping cautiously over the threshold. I immediately snatched up the negro's bow and quiver, the rattling of which made the man withdraw; and my companion, looking out, assured me that it was the mansa himself, and advised me to keep awake until the morning. I closed the door, and placed a large piece of wood behind it, and was wondering at this unexpected visit, when somebody pressed so hard against the door that the negro could scarcely keep it shut; but when I called to him to open the door, the intruder ran off as before.

September 16.—As soon as it was light the negro, at my request, went to the mansa's house and brought away my spear. He told me that the mansa was asleep, and lest this inhospitable chief should devise means to detain me, he advised me to set out before he was awake, which I immediately did, and about two o'clock reached Kamalia, a small town situated at the bottom of some rocky hills, where the inhabitants collect gold in considerable quantities.

On my arrival at Kamalia I was conducted to the house of a bushreen named Karfa Taura, the brother of him to whose hospitality I was indebted at Kinyeto. He was collecting a coffle of slaves, with a view to sell them to the Europeans on the Gambia as soon as the rains should be over. I found him sitting in his baloon, surrounded by several slatees who proposed to join the coffle. He was reading to them from an Arabic book, and inquired with a smile if I understood it. Being answered in the negative, he desired one of the slatees to fetch the little curious book which had been brought from the west country. On opening this small volume I was surprised and delighted to find it our Book of Common Prayer, and Karfa expressed great joy to hear that I could read it; for some of the slatees, who had seen the Europeans upon the coast, observing the colour of my skin (which was now become very yellow from sickness), my long beard, ragged clothes, and extreme poverty, were unwilling to admit that I was a white man, and told Karfa that they suspected I was some Arab in disguise. Karfa, however, perceiving that I could read this book, had no doubt concerning me, and kindly promised me every assistance in his power. At the same time he informed me that it was impossible to cross the Jallonka wilderness for many months yet to come, as no less than eight rapid rivers, he said, lay in the way. He added that he intended to set out himself for Gambia as soon as the rivers were fordable and the grass burnt, and advised me to stay and accompany him. He remarked that when a caravan of the natives could not travel through the country it was idle for a single white man to attempt it. I readily admitted that such an attempt was an act of rashness, but I assured him that I had no alternative, for, having no money to support myself, I must either beg my subsistence by travelling from place to place, or perish for want. Karfa now looked at me with great earnestness, and inquired if I could eat the common victuals of the country, assuring me he had never before seen a white man. He added that if I would remain with him until the rains were over, he would give me plenty of victuals in the meantime, and a hut to sleep in; and that after he had conducted me in safety to the Gambia, I might then make him what return I thought proper. I asked him if the value of one prime slave would satisfy him. He answered in the affirmative, and immediately ordered one of the huts to be swept for my accommodation. Thus was I delivered, by the friendly care of this benevolent negro, from a situation truly deplorable. Distress and famine pressed hard upon me. I had before me the gloomy wilds of Jallonkadoo, where the traveller sees no habitation for five successive days. I had observed at a distance the rapid course of the river Kokoro. I had almost marked out the place where I was doomed, I thought, to perish, when this friendly negro stretched out his hospitable hand for my relief.

In the hut which was appropriated for me I was provided with a mat to sleep on, an earthen jar for holding water, and a small calabash to drink out of; and Karfa sent me, from his own dwelling, two meals a day, and ordered his slaves to supply me with firewood and water. But I found that neither the kindness of Karfa nor any sort of accommodation could put a stop to the fever which weakened me, and which became every day more alarming. I endeavoured as much as possible to conceal my distress; but on the third day after my arrival, as I was going with Karfa to visit some of his friends, I found myself so faint that I could scarcely walk, and before we reached the place I staggered and fell into a pit, from which the clay had been taken to build one of the huts. Karfa endeavoured to console me with the hopes of a speedy recovery, assuring me that if I would not walk out in the wet I should soon be well. I determined to follow his advice, and confine myself to my hut, but was still tormented with the fever, and my health continued to be in a very precarious state for five ensuing weeks. Sometimes I could crawl out of the hut, and sit a few hours in the open air; at other times I was unable to rise, and passed the lingering hours in a very gloomy and solitary manner. I was seldom visited by any person except my benevolent landlord, who came daily to inquire after my health.

When the rains became less frequent, and the country began to grow dry, the fever left me, but in so debilitated a condition that I could scarcely stand upright; and it was with great difficulty that I could carry my mat to the shade of a tamarind-tree, at a short distance, to enjoy the refreshing smell of the cornfields, and delight my eyes with a prospect of the country. I had the pleasure at length to find myself in a state of convalescence, towards which the benevolent and simple manners of the negroes, and the perusal of Karfa's little volume, greatly contributed.

In the meantime many of the slatees who reside at Kamalia having spent all their money, and become in a great measure dependent upon Karfa's hospitality, beheld me with an eye of envy, and invented many ridiculous and trifling stories to lessen me in Karfa's esteem. And in the beginning of December a Serawoolli slatee, with five slaves, arrived from Sego; this man, too, spread a number of malicious reports concerning me, but Karfa paid no attention to them, and continued to show me the same kindness as formerly. As I was one day conversing with the slaves which this slatee had brought, one of them begged me to give him some victuals. I told him I was a stranger, and had none to give. He replied, "I gave you victuals when you were hungry. Have you forgot the man who brought you milk at Karrankalla? But," added he with a sigh, *the irons were not then upon my legs!*" I immediately recollected him, and begged some ground nuts from Karfa to give him, as a return for his former kindness.

In the beginning of December, Karfa proposed to complete his purchase of slaves, and for this purpose collected all the debts which were owing to him in his own country; and on the 19th, being accompanied by three slatees, he departed for Kancaba, a large town on the banks of the Niger and a great slave-market. Most of the slaves who are sold at Kancaba come from Bambarra; for Mansong, to avoid the expense and danger of keeping all his prisoners at Sego, commonly sends them in small parties to be sold at the different trading towns; and as Kancaba is much resorted to by merchants it is always well supplied with slaves, which are sent thither up the Niger in canoes. When Karfa departed from Kamalia he proposed to return in the course of a month, and during his absence I was left to the care of a good old bushreen, who acted as schoolmaster to the young people of Kamalia.

CHAPTER XX.
NEGRO CUSTOMS.

The whole of my route, both in going and returning, having been confined to a tract of country bounded nearly by the 12th and 15th parallels of latitude, the reader must imagine that I found the climate in most places extremely hot, but nowhere did I feel the heat so intense and oppressive as in the camp at Benowm, of which mention has been made in a former place. In some parts, where the country ascends into hills, the air is at all times, comparatively cool; yet none of the districts which I traversed could properly be called mountainous. About the middle of June the hot and sultry atmosphere is agitated by violent gusts of wind (called tornadoes), accompanied with thunder and rain. These usher in what is denominated "the rainy season," which continues until the month of November. During this time the diurnal rains are very heavy, and the prevailing winds are from the south-west. The termination of the rainy season is likewise attended with violent tornadoes, after which the wind shifts to the north-east, and continues to blow from that quarter during the rest of the year.

When the wind sets in from the north-east it produces a wonderful change in the face of the country. The grass soon becomes dry and withered, the rivers subside very rapidly, and many of the trees shed their leaves. About this period is commonly felt the *harmattan,* a dry and parching wind blowing from the north-east, and accompanied by a thick smoky haze, through which the sun appears of a dull red colour. This wind in passing over the great desert of Sahara acquires a very strong attraction for humidity, and parches up everything exposed to its current. It is, however, reckoned very salutary, particularly to Europeans, who generally recover their health during its continuance. I experienced immediate relief from sickness, both at Dr. Laidley's and at Kamalia, during the harmattan. Indeed, the air during the rainy season is so loaded with moisture that clothes, shoes, trunks, and everything that is not close to the fire becomes damp and mouldy, and the inhabitants may be said to live in a sort of vapour-bath; but this dry wind braces up the solids, which were before relaxed, gives a cheerful flow of spirits, and is even pleasant to respiration. Its ill effects are, that it produces chaps in the lips, and afflicts many of the natives with sore eyes.

Whenever the grass is sufficiently dry the negroes set it on fire; but in Ludamar and other Moorish countries this practice is not allowed, for it is upon the withered stubble that the Moors feed their cattle until the return of the rains. The burning the grass in Manding exhibits a scene of terrific grandeur. In the middle of the night I could see the plains and mountains, as far as my eye could reach, variegated with lines of fire, and the light, reflected on the sky, made the heavens appear in a blaze. In the daytime pillars of smoke were seen in every direction, while the birds of prey were observed hovering round the conflagration, and pouncing down upon the snakes, lizards, and other reptiles which attempted to escape from the flames. This annual burning is soon followed by a fresh and sweet verdure, and the country is thereby rendered more healthful and pleasant.

Of the most remarkable and important of the vegetable productions mention has already been made; and they are nearly the same in all the districts through which I passed. It is observable, however, that although many species of the edible roots which grow in the West India Islands are found in Africa, yet I never saw, in any part of my journey, either the sugar-cane, the coffee, or the cocoa-tree, nor could I learn, on inquiry, that they were known to the natives. The pine-apple and the thousand other delicious fruits which the industry of civilised man (improving the bounties of nature) has brought to so great perfection in the tropical climates of America, are here equally unknown. I observed, indeed, a few orange and banana trees near the month of the Gambia, but whether they were indigenous, or were formerly planted there by some of the white traders, I could not positively learn. I suspect that they were originally introduced by the Portuguese.

Concerning property in the soil, it appeared to me that the lands in native woods were considered as belonging to the king, or (where the government was not monarchical) to the state. When any individual of free condition had the means of cultivating more land than he actually possessed, he applied to the chief man of the district, who allowed him an extension of territory, on condition of forfeiture if the lands were not brought into cultivation by a given period. The condition being fulfilled, the soil became vested in the possessor, and, for ought that appeared to me, descended his heirs.

The population, however, considering the extent and fertility of the soil, and the ease with which lands are obtained, is not very great in the countries which I visited. I found many extensive and beautiful districts entirely destitute of inhabitants, and, in general, the borders of the different kingdoms were either very thinly peopled or entirely deserted. Many places are likewise unfavourable to population from being unhealthful. The swampy banks of the Gambia, the Senegal, and other rivers towards the coast, are of this description. Perhaps it is on this account chiefly that the interior countries abound more with inhabitants than the maritime districts; for all the negro nations that fell under my observation, though divided into a number of petty independent states, subsist chiefly by the same means, live nearly in the same temperature, and possess a wonderful similarity of disposition. The Mandingoes, in particular, are a very gentle race, cheerful in their dispositions, inquisitive, credulous, simple, and fond of flattery. Perhaps the most prominent defect in their character was that insurmountable propensity, which the reader must have observed to prevail in all classes of them, to steal from me the few effects I was possessed of. For this part of their conduct no complete justification can be offered, because theft is a crime in their own estimation; and it must be observed that they are not habitually and generally guilty of it towards each other.

On the other hand, as some counterbalance to this depravity in their nature, allowing it to be such, it is impossible for me to forget the disinterested charity and tender solicitude with which many of these poor heathens (from the sovereign of Sego to the poor women who received me at different times into their cottages when I was perishing of hunger) sympathised with me in my sufferings, relieved my distresses, and contributed to my safety. This acknowledgment, however, is perhaps more particularly due to the female part of the nation. Among the men, as the reader must have seen, my reception, though generally kind, was sometimes otherwise. It varied according to the various tempers of those to whom I made application. The hardness of avarice in some, and the blindness of bigotry in others, had closed up the avenues to compassion; but I do not recollect a single instance of hard-heartedness towards me in the women. In all my wanderings and wretchedness I found them uniformly kind and compassionate; and I can truly say, as my predecessor Mr. Ledyard has eloquently said before me, "To a woman I never addressed myself in the language of decency and friendship without receiving a decent and friendly answer. If I was hungry or thirsty, wet or sick, they did not hesitate, like the men, to perform a generous action. In so free and so kind a manner did they contribute to my relief, that if I was dry, I drank the sweetest draught, and if hungry, I ate the coarsest morsel with a double relish."

It is surely reasonable to suppose that the soft and amiable sympathy of nature, which was thus spontaneously manifested towards me in my distress, is displayed by these poor people, as occasion requires, much more strongly towards persons of their own nation and neighbourhood, and especially when the objects of their compassion are endeared to them by the ties of consanguinity. Accordingly the maternal affection (neither suppressed by the restraints nor diverted by the solicitudes of civilised life) is everywhere conspicuous among them, and creates a correspondent return of tenderness in the child. An illustration of this has been already given. "Strike me," said my attendant, "but do not curse my mother." The same sentiment I found universally to prevail, and observed in all parts of Africa that the greatest affront which could be offered to a negro was to reflect on her who gave him birth.

It is not strange that this sense of filial duty and affection among the negroes should be less ardent towards the father than the mother. The system of polygamy, while it weakens the father's attachment by dividing it among the children of different wives, concentrates all the mother's jealous tenderness to one point—the protection of her own offspring. I perceived with great satisfaction, too, that the maternal solicitude extended, not only to the growth and security of the person, but also, in a certain degree, to the improvement of the mind of the infant; for one of the first lessons in which the Mandingo women instruct their children is *the practice of truth*. The reader will probably recollect the case of the unhappy mother whose son was murdered by the Moorish banditti at Funingkedy. Her only consolation in her uttermost distress was the reflection that the poor boy, in the course of his blameless life, *had never told a lie*. Such testimony from a fond mother on such an occasion must have operated powerfully on the youthful part of the surrounding spectators. It was at once a tribute of praise to the deceased and a lesson to the living.

The negro women suckle their children until they are able to walk of themselves. Three years' nursing is not uncommon, and during this period the husband devotes his whole attention to his other wives. To this practice it is owing, I presume, that the family of each wife is seldom very numerous. Few women have more than five or six children. As soon as an infant is able to walk it is permitted to run about with great freedom. The mother is not over solicitous to preserve it from slight falls and other trifling accidents. A little practice soon enables a child to take care of itself, and experience acts the part of a nurse. As they advance in life the girls are taught to spin cotton and to beat corn, and are instructed in other domestic duties; and the boys are employed in the labours of the field. Both sexes, whether bushreens or kafirs, on attaining the age of puberty, are circumcised. This painful operation is not considered by the kafirs so much in the light of a religious ceremony as a matter of convenience and utility. They have, indeed, a superstitious notion that it contributes to render the marriage state prolific. The operation is performed upon several young people at the same time, all of whom are exempted from every sort of labour for two months afterwards. During this period they form a society called *solimana*. They visit the towns and villages in the neighbourhood, where they dance and sing, and are well treated by the inhabitants. I had frequently, in the course of my journey, observed parties of this description, but they were all males. I had, however, an opportunity of seeing a female *solimana* at Kamalia.

In the course of this celebration it frequently happens that some of the young women get married. If a man takes a fancy to any one of them, it is not considered as absolutely necessary that he should make an overture to the girl herself. The first object is to agree with the parents concerning the recompense to be given them for the loss of the company and services of their daughter. The value of two slaves is a common price, unless the girl is thought very handsome, in which case the parents will raise their demand very considerably. If the lover is rich enough, and willing to give the sum demanded, he then communicates his wishes to the damsel; but her consent is by no means necessary to the match, for if the parents agree to it and eat a few *kolla*-nuts, which are represented by the suitor as an earnest of the bargain, the young lady must either have the man of their choice or continue unmarried, for she cannot afterwards be given to another. If the parents should attempt it, the lover is then authorised by the laws of the country to seize upon the girl as his slave. When the day for celebrating the nuptials is fixed on, a select number of people are invited to be present at the wedding—a bullock or goat is killed, and great plenty of victuals is dressed for the occasion. As soon as it is dark the bride is conducted into a hut, where a company of matrons assist in arranging the wedding-dress, which is always white cotton, and is put on in such a manner as to conceal the bride from head to foot. Thus arrayed, she is seated upon a mat in the middle of the floor, and the old women place themselves in a circle round her. They then give her a series of instructions, and point out, with great propriety, what ought to be her future conduct in life. This scene of instruction, however, is frequently interrupted by girls, who amuse the company with songs and dances, which are rather more remarkable for their gaiety than delicacy. While the bride remains within the hut with the women the bridegroom devotes his attention to the guests of both sexes, who assemble without doors, and by distributing among them small presents of kolla-nuts, and seeing that every one partakes of the good cheer which is provided, he contributes much to the general hilarity of the evening. When supper is ended, the company spend the remainder of the night in singing and dancing, and seldom separate until daybreak. About midnight the bride is privately conducted by the women into the hut which is to be her future residence, and the bridegroom, upon a signal given, retires from his company.

The negroes, as hath been frequently observed, whether Mohammedan or pagan, allow a plurality of wives. The Mohammedans alone are by their religion confined to four, and as the husband commonly pays a great price for each, he requires from all of them the utmost deference and submission, and treats them more like hired servants than companions. They have, however, the management of domestic affairs, and each in rotation is mistress of the household, and has the care of dressing the victuals, overlooking the female slaves, etc. But though the African husbands are possessed of great authority over their wives I did not observe that in general they treat them with cruelty, neither did I perceive that mean jealousy in their dispositions which is so prevalent among the Moors. They permit their wives to partake of all public diversions, and this indulgence is seldom abused, for though the negro women are very cheerful and frank in their behaviour, they are by no means given to intrigue—I believe that instances of conjugal infidelity are not common. When the wives quarrel among themselves—a circumstance which, from the nature of their situation, must frequently happen—the husband decides between them, and sometimes finds it necessary to administer a little corporal chastisement before tranquillity can be restored. But if any one of the ladies complains to the chief of the town that her husband has unjustly punished her, and shown an undue partiality to some other of his wives, the affair is brought to a public trial. In these palavers, however, which are conducted chiefly by married men, I was informed that the complaint of the wife is not always considered in a very serious light, and the complainant herself is sometimes convicted of strife and contention and left without remedy. If she murmurs at the decision of the court the magic rod of Mumbo Jumbo soon puts an end to the business.

The children of the Mandingoes are not always named after their relations, but frequently in consequence of some remarkable occurrence. Thus my landlord at Kamalia was called *Karfa*, a word signifying *to replace*, because he was born shortly after the death of one of his brothers. Other names are descriptive of good or bad qualities—as *Modi*, a good man; *Fadibba*, father of the town, etc. Indeed, the very names of their towns have something descriptive in them, as *Sibidooloo*, the town of ciboa-trees; *Kenneyeto*, victuals here; *Dosita*, lift your spoon. Others appear to be given by way of reproach—as *Bammakoo*, wash a crocodile; *Karrankalla*, no cup to drink from, etc. A child is named when it is seven or eight days old. The ceremony commences by shaving the infant's head; and a dish culled *dega*, made of pounded corn and sour milk, is prepared for the guests. If the parents are rich, a sheep or goat is commonly added. The feast is called *ding koon lee* (the child's head-shaving). During my stay at Kamalia I was present at four different feasts of this kind, and the ceremony was the same in each, whether the child belonged to a bushreen or a kafir. The schoolmaster, who officiated as priest on those occasions, and who is necessarily a bushreen, first said a long prayer over the dega, during which every person present took hold of the brim of the calabash with his right hand. After this the schoolmaster took the child in his arms and said a second prayer, in which he repeatedly solicited the blessing of God upon the child and upon all the company. When this prayer was ended he whispered a few sentences in the child's ear and spat three times in its face, after which he pronounced its name aloud, and returned the infant to the mother. [80] This part of the ceremony being ended, the father of the child divided the dega into a number of balls, one of which he distributed to every person present; and inquiry was then made if any person in the town was dangerously sick, it being usual in such cases to send the party a large portion of the dega, which is thought to possess great medical virtues.

Among the negroes every individual, besides his own proper name, has likewise a *kontong*, or surname, to denote the family or clan to which he belongs. Some of these families are very numerous and powerful. It is impossible to enumerate the various *kontongs* which are found in different parts of the country, though the knowledge of many of them is of great service to the traveller; for as every negro plumes himself upon the importance or the antiquity of his clan, he is much flattered when he is addressed by his kontong.

Salutations among the negroes to each other when they meet are always observed, but those in most general use among the kafirs are, "*Abbe haeretto*," "'*E ning seni*," "*Anawari*," etc., all of which have nearly the same meaning, and signify "Are you well?" or to that effect. There are likewise salutations which are used at different times of the day, as "*E ning somo*" ("Good morning"), etc. The general answer to all salutations is to repeat the kontong of the person who salutes, or else to repeat the salutation itself, first pronouncing the word *marhaba* ("My friend").

CHAPTER XXI.
RELIGIOUS BELIEFS AND INDUSTRIES
OF THE MANDINGOES.

The Mandingoes and, I believe, the negroes in general, have no artificial method of dividing time. They calculate the years by the number of *rainy seasons*. They portion the year into *moons*, and reckon the days by so many suns. The day they divide into morning, midday, and evening; and farther subdivide it, when necessary, by pointing to the sun's place in the heavens. I frequently inquired of some of them what became of the sun during the night, and whether we should see the same sun, or a different one, in the morning; but I found that they considered the question as very childish. The subject appeared to them as placed beyond the reach of human investigation—they had never indulged a conjecture, nor formed any hypothesis, about the matter. The moon, by varying her form, has more attracted their attention. On the first appearance of the new moon, which they look upon to be newly created, the pagan natives, as well as Mohammedans, say a short prayer; and this seems to be the only visible adoration which the kafirs offer up to the Supreme Being. This prayer is pronounced in a whisper, the party holding up his hands before his face: its purport (as I have been assured by many different people) is to return thanks to God for His kindness through the existence of the past moon, and to solicit a continuation of His favour during that of the new one. At the conclusion they spit upon their hands and rub them over their faces. This seems to be nearly the same ceremony which prevailed among the heathens in the days of Job. [82]

Great attention, however, is paid to the changes of this luminary in its monthly course, and it is thought very unlucky to begin a journey, or any other work of consequence, in the last quarter. An eclipse, whether of the sun or moon, is supposed to be effected by witchcraft. The stars are very little regarded; and the whole study of astronomy appears to them as a useless pursuit, and attended to by such persons only as deal in magic.

Their notions of geography are equally puerile. They imagine that the world is an extended plain, the termination of which no eye has discovered—it being, they say, overhung with clouds and darkness. They describe the sea as a large river of salt water, on the farther shore of which is situated a country called *Tobaubo doo* (the land of the white people). At a distance from Tobaubo doo they describe another country, which they allege as inhabited by cannibals of gigantic size, called *komi*. This country they call *Jong sang doo* (the land where the slaves are sold). But of all countries in the world their own appears to them as the best, and their own people as the happiest, and they pity the fate of other nations, who have been placed by Providence in less fertile and less fortunate districts.

Some of the religious opinions of the negroes, though blended with the weakest credulity and superstition, are not unworthy attention. I have conversed with all ranks and conditions upon the subject of their faith, and can pronounce, without the smallest shadow of doubt, that the belief of one God and of a future state of reward and punishment is entire and universal among them. It is remarkable, however, that except on the appearance of a new moon, as before related, the pagan natives do not think it necessary to offer up prayers and supplications to the Almighty. They represent the Deity, indeed, as the creator and preserver of all things, but in general they consider Him as a being so remote and of so exalted a nature that it is idle to imagine the feeble supplications of wretched mortals can reverse the decrees and change the purposes of unerring wisdom. If they are asked for what reason then do they offer up a prayer on the appearance of the new moon, the answer is, that custom has made it necessary, they do it because their fathers did it before them. Such is the blindness of unassisted nature! The concerns of this world, they believe, are committed by the Almighty to the superintendence and direction of subordinate spirits, over whom they suppose that certain magical ceremonies have great influence. A white fowl suspended to the branch of a particular tree, a snake's head or a few handfuls of fruit are offerings which ignorance and superstition frequently present, to deprecate the wrath, or to conciliate the favour, of these tutelary agents. But it is not often that the negroes make their religious opinions the subject of conversation; when interrogated in particular concerning their ideas of a future state, they express themselves with great reverence, but endeavour to shorten the discussion by observing, *"Mo o mo inta allo"* ("No man knows anything about it"). They are content, they say, to follow the precepts and examples of their forefathers through the various vicissitudes of life, and when this world presents no objects of enjoyment or of comfort they seem to look with anxiety towards another, which they believe will be better suited to their natures, but concerning which they are far from indulging vain and delusive conjectures.

The Mandingoes seldom attain extreme old age. At forty most of them become grey-haired and covered with wrinkles, and but few of them survive the age of fifty-five or sixty. They calculate the years of their lives, as I have already observed, by the number of rainy seasons (there being but one such in the year), and distinguish each year by a particular name, founded on some remarkable occurrence which happened in that year. Thus they say the year of the *Farbanna* war—the year of the *Kaarta war*—the year on which *Gadou was plundered*, etc., etc.; and I have no doubt that the year 1796 will in many places be distinguished by the name of *tobaubo tambi sang* (the year the white man passed), as such an occurrence would naturally form an epoch in their traditional history.

But notwithstanding that longevity is uncommon among them, it appeared to me that their diseases are but few in number. Their simple diet and active way of life preserve them from many of those disorders which embitter the days of luxury and idleness. Fevers and fluxes are the most common and the most fatal. For these they generally apply saphies to different parts of the body, and perform a great many other superstitious ceremonies—some of which are indeed well calculated to inspire the patient with the hope of recovery, and divert his mind from brooding over his own danger—but I have sometimes observed among them a more systematic mode of treatment. On the first attack of a fever, when the patient complains of cold, he is frequently placed in a sort of vapour-bath. This is done by spreading branches of the *nauclea orientalis* upon hot wood embers, and laying the patient upon them, wrapped up in a large cotton cloth. Water is then sprinkled upon the branches, which, descending to the hot embers, soon covers the patient with a cloud of vapour, in which he is allowed to remain until the embers are almost extinguished. This practice commonly produces a profuse perspiration, and wonderfully relieves the sufferer.

For the dysentery they use the bark of different trees reduced to powder and mixed with the patient's food; but this practice is in general very unsuccessful.

The other diseases which prevail among the negroes are the *yaws*, the *elephantiasis*, and a *leprosy* of the very worst kind. This last-mentioned complaint appears at the beginning in scurfy spots upon different parts of the body, which finally settle upon the hands or feet, where the skin becomes withered, and, cracks in many places. At length the ends of the fingers swell and ulcerate, the discharge is acrid and fetid, the nails drop off, and the bones of the fingers become carious, and separate at the joints. In this manner the disease continues to spread, frequently until the patient loses all his fingers and toes. Even the hands and feet are sometimes destroyed by this inveterate malady, to which the negroes give the name of *balla ou* (incurable).

The *guinea worm* is likewise very common in certain places, especially at the commencement of the rainy season. The negroes attribute this disease, which has been described by many writers, to bad water, and allege that the people who drink from wells are more subject to it than those who drink from streams. To the same cause they attribute the swelling of the glands of the neck (*goitres*), which are very common in some parts of Bambarra. I observed also, in the interior countries, a few instances of simple *gonorrhœa*, but never the confirmed *lues*. On the whole, it appeared to me that the negroes are better surgeons than physicians. I found them very successful in their management of fractures and dislocations, and their splints and bandages are simple and easily removed. The patient is laid upon a soft mat, and the fractured limb is frequently bathed with cold water. All abscesses they open with the actual cautery, and the dressings are composed of either soft leaves, shea butter, or cow's dung, as the case seems in their judgment to require. Towards the coast, where a supply of European lancets can be procured, they sometimes perform phlebotomy, and in cases of local inflammation a curious sort of cupping is practised. This operation is performed by making incisions in the part, and applying to it a bullock's horn with a small hole in the end. The operator then takes a piece of bee's wax in his mouth, and, putting his lips to the hole, extracts the air from the horn, and by a dexterous use of his tongue stops up the hole with the wax. This method is found to answer the purpose, and in general produces a plentiful discharge.

When a person of consequence dies, the relations and neighbours meet together and manifest their sorrow by loud and dismal howlings. A bullock or goat is killed for such persons as come to assist at the funeral, which generally takes place in the evening of the same day on which the party died. The negroes have no appropriate burial-places, and frequently dig the grave in the floor of the deceased's hut, or in the shade of a favourite tree. The body is dressed in white cotton, and wrapped up in a mat. It is carried to the grave in the dusk of the evening by the relations. If the grave is without the walls of the town a number of prickly bushes are laid upon it to prevent the wolves from digging up the body; but I never observed that any stone was placed over the grave as a monument or memorial.

Of their music and dances some account has incidentally been given in different parts of my journal. On the first of these heads I have now to add a list of their musical instruments, the principal of which are—the *koonting*, a sort of guitar with three strings; the *korro*, a large harp with eighteen strings; the *simbing*, a small harp with seven strings; the *balafou*, an instrument composed of twenty pieces of hard wood of different lengths, with the shells of gourds hung underneath to increase the sound; the *tangtang*, a drum open at the lower end; and, lastly, the *tabala*, a large drum, commonly used to spread an alarm through the country. Besides these, they make use of small flutes, bow-strings, elephants' teeth and bells; and at all their dances and concerts *clapping of hands* appears to constitute a necessary part of the chorus.

With the love of music is naturally connected a taste for poetry; and fortunately for the poets of Africa they are in a great measure exempted from that neglect and indigence which in more polished countries commonly attend the votaries of the Muses. They consist of two classes; the most numerous are the *singing men*, called *jilli kea*, mentioned in a former part of my narrative. One or more of these may be found in every town. They sing extempore songs in honour of their chief men, or any other persons who are willing to give "solid pudding for empty praise." But a nobler part of their office is to recite the historical events of their country; hence in war they accompany the soldiers to the field, in order, by reciting the great actions of their ancestors, to awaken in them a spirit of glorious emulation. The other class are devotees of the Mohammedan faith, who travel about the country singing devout hymns and performing religious ceremonies, to conciliate the favour of the Almighty, either in averting calamity or insuring success to any enterprise. Both descriptions of these itinerant bards are much employed and respected by the people, and very liberal contributions are made for them.

The usual diet of the negroes is somewhat different in different districts; in general the people of free condition breakfast about daybreak upon gruel made of meal and water, with a little of the fruit of the tamarind to give it an acid taste. About two o'clock in the afternoon a sort of hasty pudding, with a little shea butter, is the common meal; but the supper constitutes the principal repast, and is seldom ready before midnight. This consists almost universally of kouskous, with a small portion of animal food or shea butter mixed with it. In eating, the kafirs, as well as Mohammedans, use the right hand only.

The beverages of the pagan negroes are beer and mead, of each of which they frequently drink to excess. The Mohammedan convert drinks nothing but water. The natives of all descriptions take snuff and smoke tobacco; their pipes are made of wood, with an earthen bowl of curious workmanship. But in the interior countries the greatest of all luxuries is salt. It would appear strange to a European to see a child suck a piece of rock salt as if it were sugar. This, however, I have frequently seen, although, in the inland parts, the poorer class of inhabitants are so very rarely indulged with this precious article that to say *a man ate salt with his victuals* is the same as saying *he is a very rich man.* I have myself suffered great inconvenience from the scarcity of this article. The long use of vegetable food creates so painful a longing for salt that no words can sufficiently describe it.

The negroes in general, and the Mandingoes in particular, are considered by the whites on the coast as an indolent and inactive people—I think without reason. The nature of the climate is, indeed, unfavourable to great exertion; but surely a people cannot justly be denominated habitually indolent whose wants are supplied, not by the spontaneous productions of nature, but by their own exertions. Few people work harder, when occasion requires, than the Mandingoes; but not having many opportunities of turning to advantage the superfluous produce of their labour, they are content with cultivating as much ground only as is necessary for their own support. The labours of the field give them pretty full employment during the rains; and in the dry season the people who live in the vicinity of large rivers employ themselves in fishing. The fish are taken in wicker baskets or with small cotton nets, and are preserved by being first dried in the sun and afterwards rubbed with shea butter, to prevent them from contracting fresh moisture. Others of the natives employ themselves in hunting. Their weapons are bows and arrows; but the arrows in common use are not poisoned. [92] They are very dexterous marksmen, and will hit a lizard on a tree, or any other small object, at an amazing distance. They likewise kill guinea-fowls, partridges, and pigeons, but never on the wing. While the men are occupied in these pursuits the women are very diligent in manufacturing cotton cloth. They prepare the cotton for spinning by laying it in small quantities at a time upon a smooth stone or piece of wood, and rolling the seeds out with a thick iron spindle; and they spin it with the distaff. The thread is not fine, but well twisted, and makes a very durable cloth. A woman with common diligence will spin from six to nine garments of this cloth in one year, which, according to its fineness, will sell for a minkalli and a half or two minkallies each. [93] The weaving is performed by the men. The loom is made exactly upon the same principle as that of Europe, but so small and narrow that the web is seldom more than four inches broad. The shuttle is of the common construction, but as the thread is coarse the chamber is somewhat larger than the European.

The women dye this cloth of a rich and lasting blue colour by the following simple process:—The leaves of the indigo, when fresh gathered, are pounded in a wooden mortar, and mixed in a large earthen jar with a strong ley of wood-ashes; chamber-ley is sometimes added. The cloth is steeped in this mixture, and allowed to remain until it has acquired the proper shade. In Kaarta and Ludamar, where the indigo is not plentiful, they collect the leaves and dry them in the sun; and when they wish to use them they reduce a sufficient quantity to powder and mix it with the ley, as before mentioned.

Either way the colour is very beautiful, with a fine purple gloss, and equal in my opinion to the best Indian or European blue. This cloth is cut into various pieces and sewed into garments with needles of the natives' own making.

As the arts of weaving, dyeing, sewing, etc., may easily be acquired, those who exercise them are not considered in Africa as following any particular profession, for almost every slave can weave, and every boy can sew. The only artists who are distinctly acknowledged as such by the negroes, and who value themselves on exercising appropriate and peculiar trades, are the manufacturers of *leather* and of *iron*. The first of these are called *karrankea* (or, as the word is sometimes pronounced, *gaungay*). They are to be found in almost every town, and they frequently travel through the country in the exercise of their calling. They tan and dress leather with very great expedition, by steeping the hide first in a mixture of wood-ashes and water until it parts with the hair, and afterwards by using the pounded leaves of a tree called *goo* as an astringent. They are at great pains to render the hide as soft and pliant as possible, by rubbing it frequently between their hands and beating it upon a stone. The hides of bullocks are converted chiefly into sandals, and therefore require less care in dressing than the skins of sheep and goats, which are used for covering quivers and saphies, and in making sheaths for swords and knives, belts, pockets, and a variety of ornaments. These skins commonly are dyed of a red or yellow colour—the red by means of millet stalks reduced to powder; and the yellow by the root of a plant the name of which I have forgotten.

The manufacturers in iron are not so numerous as the *karrankeas*, but they appear to have studied their business with equal diligence. The negroes on the coast being cheaply supplied with iron from the European traders, never attempt the manufacturing of this article themselves; but in the inland parts the natives smelt this useful metal in such quantities not only to supply themselves from it with all necessary weapons and instruments, but even to make it a article of commerce with some of the neighbouring states. During my stay at Kamalia there was a smelting furnace at a short distance from the hut where I lodged, and the owner and his workmen made no secret about the manner of conducting the operation, and readily allowed me to examine the furnace, and assist them in breaking the ironstone. The furnace was a circular tower of clay, about ten feet high and three feet in diameter, surrounded in two places with withes, to prevent the clay from cracking and falling to pieces by the violence of the heat. Round the lower part, on a level with the ground—but not so low as the bottom of the furnace, which was somewhat concave—were made seven openings, into every one of which were placed three tubes of clay, and the openings again plastered up in such a manner that no air could enter the furnace but through the tubes, by the opening and shutting of which they regulated the fire. These tubes were formed by plastering a mixture of clay and grass round a smooth roller of wood, which, as soon as the clay began to harden, was withdrawn, and the tube left to dry in the sun. The ironstone which I saw was very heavy, of a dull red colour with greyish specks; it was broken into pieces about the size of a hen's egg. A bundle of dry wood was first put into the furnace, and covered with a considerable quantity of charcoal, which was brought, ready burnt, from the woods. Over this was laid a stratum of ironstone, and then another of charcoal, and so on, until the furnace was quite full. The fire was applied through one of the tubes, and blown for some time with bellows made of goats' skins. The operation went on very slowly at first, and it was some hours before the flame appeared above the furnace; but after this it burnt with great violence all the first night, and the people who attended put in at times more charcoal. On the day following the fire was not so fierce, and on the second night some of the tubes were withdrawn and the air allowed to have freer access to the furnace; but the heat was still very great, and a bluish flame rose some feet above the top of the furnace. On the third day from the commencement of the operation, all the tubes were taken out, the ends of many of them being vitrified with the heat; but the metal was not removed until some days afterwards, when the whole was perfectly cool. Part of the furnace was then taken down, and the iron appeared in the form of a large irregular mass, with pieces of charcoal adhering to it. It was sonorous; and when any portion was broken off, the fracture exhibited a granulated appearance, like broken steel. The owner informed me that many parts of this cake were useless, but still there was good iron enough to repay him for his trouble. This iron, or rather steel, is formed into various instruments by being repeatedly heated in a forge, the heat of which is urged by a pair of double bellows of a very simple construction, being made of two goats' skins the tubes from which unite before they enter the forge, and supply a constant and very regular blast. The hammer, forceps, and anvil are all very simple, and the workmanship (particularly in the formation of knives and spears) is not destitute of merit. The iron, indeed, is hard and brittle, and requires much labour before it can be made to answer the purpose.

Such is the chief information I obtained concerning the present state of arts and manufactures in those regions of Africa which I explored in my journey. I might add, though it is scarce worthy observation, that in Bambarra and Kaarta the natives make very beautiful baskets, hats, and other articles, both for use and ornament, from rushes, which they stain of different colours; and they contrive also to cover their calabashes with interwoven cane, dyed in the same manner.

CHAPTER XXII.
WAR AND SLAVERY.

A state of subordination and certain inequalities of rank and condition are inevitable in every stage of civil society; but when the subordination is carried to so great a length that the persons and services of one part of the community are entirely at the disposal of another part, it may then be denominated a state of slavery, and in this condition of life a great body of the negro inhabitants of Africa have continued from the most early period of their history, with this aggravation, that their children are born to no other inheritance.

The slaves in Africa, I suppose, are nearly in the proportion of three to one to the freemen. They claim no reward for their services except food and clothing, and are treated with kindness or severity, according to the good or bad disposition of their masters. Custom, however, has established certain rules with regard to the treatment of slaves, which it is thought dishonourable to violate. Thus the domestic slaves, or such as are born in a man's own house, are treated with more lenity than those which are purchased with money. The authority of the master over the domestic slave, as I have elsewhere observed, extends only to reasonable correction; for the master cannot sell his domestic, without having first brought him to a public trial before the chief men of the place. But these restrictions on the power of the master extend not to the care of prisoners taken in war, nor to that of slaves purchased with money. All these unfortunate beings are considered as strangers and foreigners, who have no right to the protection of the law, and may be treated with severity, or sold to a stranger, according to the pleasure of their owners. There are, indeed, regular markets, where slaves of this description are bought and sold, and the value of a slave, in the eye of an African purchaser, increases in proportion to his distance from his native kingdom: for when slaves are only a few days' journey from the place of their nativity they frequently effect their escape; but when one or more kingdoms intervene, escape being more difficult, they are more readily reconciled to their situation. On this account the unhappy slave is frequently transferred from one dealer to another, until he has lost all hopes of returning to his native kingdom. The slaves which are purchased by the Europeans on the coast are chiefly of this description. A few of them are collected in the petty wars, hereafter to be described, which take place near the coast, but by far the greater number are brought down in large caravans from the inland countries, of which many are unknown, even by name, to the Europeans. The slaves which are thus brought from the interior may be divided into two distinct classes—first, such as were slaves from their birth, having been born of enslaved mothers; secondly, such as were born free, but who afterwards, by whatever means, became slaves. Those of the first description are by far the most numerous, for prisoners taken in war (at least such as are taken in open and declared war, when one kingdom avows hostilities against another) are generally of this description. The comparatively small proportion of free people to the enslaved throughout Africa has already been noticed: and it must be observed that men of free condition have many advantages over the slaves, even in war time. They are in general better armed, and well mounted, and can either fight or escape with some hopes of success; but the slaves, who have only their spears and bows, and of whom great numbers are loaded with baggage, become an easy prey. Thus when Mansong, king of Bambarra, made war upon Kaarta (as I have related in a former chapter), he took in one day nine hundred prisoners, of which number not more than seventy were freemen. This account I received from Daman Jumma, who had thirty slaves at Kemmoo, all of whom were made prisoners by Mansong. Again, when a freeman is taken prisoner his friends will sometimes ransom him by giving two slaves in exchange; but when a slave is taken, he has no hopes of such redemption. To these disadvantages, it is to be added that the slatees, who purchase slaves in the interior countries and carry them down to the coast for sale, constantly prefer such as have been in that condition of life from their infancy, well knowing that these have been accustomed to hunger and fatigue, and are better able to sustain the hardships of a long and painful journey than freemen; and on their reaching the coast, if no opportunity offers of selling them to advantage, they can easily be made to maintain themselves by their labour; neither are they so apt to attempt making their escape as those who have once tasted the blessings of freedom.

Slaves of the second description generally become such by one or other of the following causes:—1, captivity; 2, famine; 3, insolvency; 4, crimes. A freeman may, by the established customs of Africa, become a slave by being taken in war. War is of all others the most productive source, and was probably the origin, of slavery; for when one nation had taken from another a greater number of captives than could be exchanged on equal terms, it is natural to suppose that the conquerors, finding it inconvenient to maintain their prisoners, would compel them to labour—at first, perhaps, only for their own support, but afterwards to support their masters. Be this as it may, it is a known fact that prisoners of war in Africa are the slaves of the conquerors; and when the weak or unsuccessful warrior begs for mercy beneath the uplifted spear of his opponent, he gives up at the same time his claim to liberty, and purchases his life at the expense of his freedom.

In a country divided into a thousand petty states, mostly independent and jealous of each other, where every freeman is accustomed to arms and fond of military achievements, where the youth, who has practised the bow and spear from his infancy, longs for nothing so much as an opportunity to display his valour, it is natural to imagine that wars frequently originate from very frivolous provocation. When one nation is more powerful than another, pretext is seldom wanting for commencing hostilities. Thus the war between Kajaaga and Kasson was occasioned by the detention of a fugitive slave; that between Bambarra and Kaarta by the loss of a few cattle. Other cases of the same nature perpetually occur in which the folly or mad ambition of their princes and the zeal of their religious enthusiasts give full employment to the scythe of desolation.

The wars of Africa are of two kinds, which are distinguished by different appellations; that species which bears the greatest resemblance to our European contests is denominated *killi*, a word signifying "to call out," because such wars are openly avowed and previously declared. Wars of this description in Africa commonly terminate, however, in the course of a single campaign. A battle is fought—the vanquished seldom think of rallying again—the whole inhabitants become panic-struck, and the conquerors have only to bind the slaves and carry off their plunder and their victims. Such of the prisoners as, through age or infirmity, are unable to endure fatigue, or are found unfit for sale, are considered as useless, and, I have no doubt, are frequently put to death. The same fate commonly awaits a chief or any other person who has taken a very distinguished part in the war. And here it may be observed that, notwithstanding this exterminating system, it is surprising to behold how soon an African town is rebuilt and repeopled. The circumstance arises probably from this: that their pitched battles are few—the weakest know their own situation, and seek safety in flight. When their country has been desolated, and their ruined towns and villages deserted by the enemy, such of the inhabitants as have escaped the *sword* and the *chain* generally return, though with cautious steps, to the place of their nativity—for it seems to be the universal wish of mankind to spend the evening of their days where they passed their infancy. The poor negro feels this desire in its full force. To him no water is sweet but what is drawn from his own well, and no tree has so cool and pleasant a shade as the *tabba* tree [104] of his native village. When war compels him to abandon the delightful spot in which he first drew his breath, and seek for safety in some other kingdom, his time is spent in talking about the country of his ancestors; and no sooner is peace restored than he turns his back upon the land of strangers, rebuilds with haste his fallen walls, and exults to see the smoke ascend from his native village.

The other species of African warfare is distinguished by the appellation of *tegria* (plundering, or stealing). It arises from a sort of hereditary feud which the inhabitants of one nation or district bear towards another. No immediate cause of hostility is assigned, or notice of attack given, but the inhabitants of each watch every opportunity to plunder and distress the objects of their animosity by predatory excursions. These are very common, particularly about the beginning of the dry season, when the labour of the harvest is over and provisions are plentiful. Schemes of vengeance are then meditated. The chief man surveys the number and activity of his vassals as they brandish their spears at festivals, and, elated with his own importance, turns his whole thoughts towards revenging some depredation or insult which either he or his ancestors may have received from a neighbouring state.

Wars of this description are generally conducted with great secrecy. A few resolute individuals, headed by some person of enterprise and courage, march quietly through the woods, surprise in the night some unprotected village, and carry off the inhabitants and their effects before their neighbours can come to their assistance. One morning during my stay at Kamalia we were all much alarmed by a party of this kind. The king of Fooladoo's son, with five hundred horsemen, passed secretly through the woods a little to the southward of Kamalia, and on the morning following plundered three towns belonging to Madigai, a powerful chief in Jallonkadoo.

The success of this expedition encouraged the governor of Bangassi, a town in Fooladoo, to make a second inroad upon another part of the same country. Having assembled about two hundred of his people, he passed the river Kokoro in the night, and carried off a great number of prisoners. Several of the inhabitants who had escaped these attacks were afterwards seized by the Mandingoes as they wandered about in the woods or concealed themselves in the glens and strong places of the mountains.

These plundering excursions always produced speedy retaliation: and when large parties cannot be collected for this purpose, a few friends will combine together and advance into the enemy's country, with a view to plunder or carry off the inhabitants. A single individual has been known to take his bow and quiver and proceed in like manner. Such an attempt is doubtless in him an act of rashness; but when it is considered that in one of these predatory wars he has probably been deprived of his child or his nearest relation, his situation will rather call for pity than censure. The poor sufferer, urged on by the feelings of domestic or paternal attachment and the ardour of revenge, conceals himself among the bushes until some young or unarmed person passes by. He then, tiger-like, springs upon his prey, drags his victim into the thicket, and in the night carries him off as a slave.

When a negro has, by means like these, once fallen into the hands of his enemies, he is either retained as the slave of his conqueror, or bartered into a distant kingdom; for an African, when he has once subdued his enemy, will seldom give him an opportunity of lifting up his hand against him at a future period. A conqueror commonly disposes of his captives according to the rank which they held in their native kingdom. Such of the domestic slaves as appear to be of a mild disposition, and particularly the young women, are retained as his own slaves. Others that display marks of discontent are disposed of in a distant country; and such of the freemen or slaves as have taken an active part in the war are either sold to the slatees or put to death. War, therefore, is certainly the most general and most productive source of slavery, and the desolations of war often (but not always) produce the second cause of slavery, *famine*; in which case a freeman becomes a slave to avoid a greater calamity.

Perhaps, by a philosophic and reflecting mind, death itself would scarcely be considered as a greater calamity than slavery; but the poor negro, when fainting with hunger, thinks like Esau of old, "Behold, I am at the point to die, and what profit shall this birthright do to me?" There are many instances of freemen voluntarily surrendering up their liberty to save their lives. During a great scarcity, which lasted for three years, in the countries of the Gambia, great numbers of people became slaves in this manner. Dr. Laidley assured me that at that time many freemen came and begged, with great earnestness, *to be put upon his slave-chain*, to save them from perishing of hunger. Large families are very often exposed to absolute want; and as the parents have almost unlimited authority over their children, it frequently happens, in all parts of Africa, that some of the latter are sold to purchase provisions for the rest of the family. When I was at Jarra, Daman Jumma pointed out to me three young slaves whom he had purchased in this manner. I have already related another instance which I saw at Wonda; and I was informed that in Fooladoo, at that time, it was a very common practice.

The third cause of slavery is *insolvency*. Of all the offences (if insolvency may be so called) to which the laws of Africa have affixed the punishment of slavery, this is the most common. A negro trader commonly contracts debts on some mercantile speculation, either from his neighbours, to purchase such articles as will sell to advantage in a distant market, or from the European traders on the coast—payment to be made in a given time. In both cases the situation of the adventurer is exactly the same. If he succeeds, he may secure an independency: if he is unsuccessful, his person and services are at the disposal of another; for in Africa, not only the effects of the insolvent, but even the insolvent himself, is sold to satisfy the lawful demands of his creditors. [109]

The fourth cause above enumerated is, *the commission of crimes on which the laws of the country affix slavery as a punishment*. In Africa the only offences of this class are murder, adultery, and witchcraft, and I am happy to say that they did not appear to me to be common. In cases of murder, I was informed that the nearest relation of the deceased had it in his power, after conviction, either to kill the offender with his own hand or sell him into slavery. When adultery occurs, it is generally left to the option of the person injured either to sell the culprit or accept such a ransom for him as he may think equivalent to the injury he has sustained. By witchcraft is meant pretended magic, by which the lives or healths of persons are affected; in other words, it is the administering of poison. No trial for this offence, however, came under my observation while I was in Africa, and I therefore suppose that the crime and its punishment occur but very seldom.

When a freeman has become a slave by any one of the causes before mentioned, he generally continues so for life, and his children (if they are born of an enslaved mother) are brought up in the same state of servitude. There are, however, a few instances of slaves obtaining their freedom, and sometimes even with the consent of their masters, as by performing some singular piece of service, or by going to battle and bringing home two slaves as a ransom; but the common way of regaining freedom is by escape, and when slaves have once set their minds on running away they often succeed. Some of them will wait for years before an opportunity presents itself, and during that period show no signs of discontent. In general, it may be remarked that slaves who come from a hilly country and have been much accustomed to hunting and travel, are more apt to attempt to make their escape than such as are born in a flat country and have been employed in cultivating the land.

Such are the general outlines of that system of slavery which prevails in Africa, and it is evident, from its nature and extent, that it is a system of no modern date. It probably had its origin in the remote ages of antiquity, before the Mohammedans explored a path across the desert. How far it is maintained and supported by the slave traffic which for two hundred years the nations of Europe have carried on with the natives of the coast, it is neither within my province nor in my power to explain. If my sentiments should be required concerning the effect which a discontinuance of that commerce would produce on the manners of the natives, I should have no hesitation in observing that, in the present unenlightened state of their minds, my opinion is, the effect would neither be so extensive nor beneficial as many wise and worthy persons fondly expect.

CHAPTER XXIII.
GOLD AND IVORY.

Those valuable commodities, gold and ivory (the next objects of our inquiry), have probably been found in Africa from the first ages of the world. They are reckoned among its most important productions in the earliest records of its history.

It has been observed that gold is seldom or never discovered except in *mountainous* and *barren* countries—nature, it is said, thus making amends in one way for her penuriousness in the other. This, however, is not wholly true. Gold is found in considerable quantities throughout every part of Manding, a country which is indeed hilly, but cannot properly be called *mountainous*, much less *barren*. It is also found in great plenty in Jallonkadoo (particularly about Boori), another hilly, but by no means an unfertile, country. It is remarkable that in the place last mentioned (Boori), which is situated about four days' journey to the south-west of Kamalia, the salt market is often supplied at the same time with rock-salt from the Great Desert and sea-salt from the Rio Grande; the price of each, at this distance from its source, being nearly the same. And the dealers in each, whether Moors from the north or negroes from the west, are invited thither by the same motives—that of bartering their salt for gold.

The gold of Manding, so far as I could learn, is never found in any matrix or vein, but always in small grains nearly in a pure state, from the size of a pin's head to that of a pea, scattered through a large body of sand or clay, and in this state it is called by the Mandingoes *sanoo munko* (gold powder). It is, however, extremely probable, by what I could learn of the situation of the ground, that most of it has originally been washed down by repeated torrents from the neighbouring hills. The manner in which it is collected is nearly as follows:—

About the beginning of December, when the harvest is over and the streams and torrents have greatly subsided, the mansa or chief of the town appoints a day to begin *sanoo koo* (gold-washing), and the women are sure to have themselves in readiness by the time appointed. A hoe or spade for digging up the sand, two or three calabashes for washing it in, and a few quills for containing the gold dust, are all the implements necessary for the purpose. On the morning of their departure a bullock is killed for the first day's entertainment, and a number of prayers and charms are used to insure success, for a failure on that day is thought a bad omen.

The mansa of Kamalia, with fourteen of his people, were, I remember, so much disappointed in their first day's washing that very few of them had resolution to persevere, and the few that did had but very indifferent success: which indeed is not much to be wondered at, for instead of opening some untried place they continued to dig and wash in the same spot where they had dug and washed for years, and where, of course, but few large grains could be left.

The washing of the sands of the streams is by far the easiest way of obtaining the gold dust; but in most places the sands have been so narrowly searched before, that unless the stream takes some new course the gold is found but in small quantities. While some of the party are busied in washing the sands, others employ themselves farther up the torrent, where the rapidity of the stream has carried away all the clay, sand, etc., and left nothing but small pebbles. The search among these is a very troublesome task. I have seen women who have had the skin worn off the tops of their fingers in this employment. Sometimes, however, they are rewarded by finding pieces of gold, which they call *sanoo birro* (gold stones), that amply repay them for their trouble. A woman and her daughter, inhabitants of Kamalia, found in one day two pieces of this kind; one of five drachms and the other of three drachms weight. But the most certain and profitable mode of washing is practised in the height of the dry season, by digging a deep pit, like a draw-well, near some hill which has previously been discovered to contain gold. The pit is dug with small spades or corn-hoes, and the earth is drawn up in large calabashes. As the negroes dig through the different strata of clay or sand, a calabash or two of each is washed by way of experiment; and in this manner the labourers proceed, until they come to a stratum containing gold, or until they are obstructed by rocks, or inundated by water. In general, when they come to a stratum of fine reddish sand, with small black specks therein, they find gold in some proportion or other, and send up large calabashes full of the sand for the women to wash; for though the pit is dug by the men, the gold is always washed by the women, who are accustomed from their infancy to a similar operation in separating the husks of corn from the meal.

As I never descended into any one of these pits, I cannot say in what manner they are worked underground. Indeed, the situation in which I was placed made it necessary for me to be cautious not to incur the suspicion of the natives by examining too far into the riches of their country; but the manner of separating the gold from the sand is very simple, and is frequently performed by the women in the middle of the town; for when the searchers return, from the valleys in the evening, they commonly bring with them each a calabash or two of sand, to be washed by such of the females as remain at home. The operation is simply as follows:—

A portion of sand or clay (for the gold is sometimes found in a brown-coloured clay) is put into a large calabash and mixed with a sufficient quantity of water. The woman whose office it is, then shakes the calabash in such a manner as to mix the sand and water together, and give the whole a rotatory motion—at first gently, but afterwards more quickly, until a small portion of sand and water, at every revolution, flies over the brim of the calabash. The sand thus separated is only the coarsest particles mixed with a little muddy water. After the operation has been continued for some time, the sand is allowed to subside, and the water poured off; a portion of coarse sand, which is now uppermost in the calabash, is removed by the hand, and, fresh water being added, the operation is repeated until the water comes off almost pure. The woman now takes a second calabash, and shakes the sand and water gently from the one to the other, reserving that portion of sand which is next the bottom of the calabash, and which is most likely to contain the gold. This small quantity is mixed with some pure water, and, being moved about in the calabash, is carefully examined. If a few particles of gold are picked out, the contents of the other calabash are examined in the same manner, but in general the party is well contented if she can obtain three or four grains from the contents of both calabashes. Some women, however, by long practice, become so well acquainted with the nature of the sand, and the mode of washing it, that they will collect gold where others cannot find a single particle. The gold dust is kept in quills stopped up with cotton; and the washers are fond of displaying a number of these quills in their hair. Generally speaking, if a person uses common diligence in a proper soil, it is supposed that as much gold may be collected by him in the course of the dry season as is equal to the value of two slaves.

Thus simple is the process by which the negroes obtain gold in Manding; and it is evident from this account that the country contains a considerable portion of this precious metal, for many of the smaller particles must necessarily escape the observation of the naked eye; and as the natives generally search the sands of streams at a considerable distance from the hills, and consequently far removed from the mines where the gold was originally produced, the labourers are sometimes but ill-paid for their trouble. Minute particles only of this heavy metal can be carried by the current to any considerable distance; the larger must remain deposited near the original source from whence they came. Were the gold-bearing streams to be traced to their fountains, and the hills from whence they spring properly examined, the sand in which the gold is there deposited would no doubt be found to contain particles of a much larger size; and even the small grains might be collected to considerable advantage by the use of quicksilver and other improvements, with which the natives are at present unacquainted.

Part of this gold is converted into ornaments for the women, but in general these ornaments are more to be admired for their weight than their workmanship. They are massy and inconvenient, particularly the earrings, which are commonly so heavy as to pull down and lacerate the lobe of the ear; to avoid which, they are supported by a thong of red leather, which passes over the crown of the head from one ear to the other. The necklace displays greater fancy, and the proper arrangement of the different beads and plates of gold is the great criterion of taste and elegance. When a lady of consequence is in full dress, her gold ornaments may be worth altogether from fifty to eighty pounds sterling.

A small quantity of gold is likewise employed by the slatees in defraying the expenses of their journeys to and from the coast, but by far the greater proportion is annually carried away by the Moors in exchange for salt and other merchandise. During my stay at Kamalia, the gold collected by the different traders at that place for salt alone was nearly equal to one hundred and ninety-eight pounds sterling; and as Kamalia is but a small town, and not much resorted to by the trading Moors, this quantity must have borne a very small proportion to the gold collected at Kancaba, Kankaree, and some other large towns. The value of salt in this part of Africa is very great. One slab, about two feet and a half in length, fourteen inches in breadth, and two inches in thickness, will sometimes sell for about two pounds ten shillings sterling; and from one pound fifteen shillings to two pounds may be considered as the common price. Four of these slabs are considered as a load for an ass, and six for a bullock. The value of European merchandise in Manding varies very much according to the supply from the coast, or the dread of war in the country; but the return for such articles is commonly made in slaves. The price of a prime slave, when I was at Kamalia, was from twelve to nine minkallies, and European commodities had then nearly the following value:—

18 gun-flints, 48 leaves of tobacco, 20 charges of gunpowder, A cutlass,	one minkalli.
A musket,	from three to four minkallies.

The produce of the country and the different necessaries of life, when exchanged for gold, sold as follows:—

Common provisions for one day, the weight of one *teeleekissi* (a black bean, six of which make the weight of one minkalli); a chicken, one teeleekissi; a sheep, three teeleekissi; a bullock, one minkalli; a horse, from ten to seventeen minkallies.

The negroes weigh the gold in small balances, which they always carry about them. They make no difference, in point of value, between gold dust and wrought gold. In bartering one article for another, the person who receives the gold always weighs it with his own teeleekissi. These beans are sometimes fraudulently soaked in shea-butter to make them heavy, and I once saw a pebble ground exactly into the form of one of them; but such practices are not very common.

Having now related the substance of what occurs to my recollection concerning the African mode of obtaining gold from the earth, and its value in barter, I proceed to the next article of which I proposed to treat—namely, ivory.

Nothing creates a greater surprise among the negroes on the sea-coast than the eagerness displayed by the European traders to procure elephants' teeth, it being exceedingly difficult to make them comprehend to what use it is applied. Although they are shown knives with ivory handles, combs and toys of the same material, and are convinced that the ivory thus manufactured was originally parts of a tooth, they are not satisfied. They suspect that this commodity is more frequently converted in Europe to purposes of far greater importance, the true nature of which is studiously concealed from them, lest the price of ivory should be enhanced. They cannot, they say, easily persuade themselves that ships would be built and voyages undertaken to procure an article which had no other value than that of furnishing handles to knives, etc., when pieces of wood would answer the purpose equally well.

Elephants are very numerous in the interior of Africa, but they appear to be a distinct species from those found in Asia. Blumenbach, in his figures of objects of natural history, has given good drawings of a grinder of each, and the variation is evident. M. Cuvier also has given in the *Magasin Encyclopédique* a clear account of the difference between them. As I never examined the Asiatic elephant, I have chosen rather to refer to those writers than advance this as an opinion of my own. It has been said that the African elephant is of a less docile nature than the Asiatic, and incapable of being tamed. The negroes certainly do not at present tame them; but when we consider that the Carthaginians had always tame elephants in their armies, and actually transported some of them to Italy in the course of the Punic wars, it seems more likely that they should have possessed the art of taming their own elephants than have submitted to the expense of bringing such vast animals from Asia. Perhaps the barbarous practice of hunting the African elephants for the sake of their teeth has rendered them more untractable and savage than they were found to be in former times.

The greater part of the ivory which is sold on the Gambia and Senegal rivers is brought from the interior country. The lands towards the coast are too swampy and too much intersected with creeks and rivers for so bulky an animal as the elephant to travel through without being discovered; and when once the natives discern the marks of his feet in the earth, the whole village is up in arms. The thoughts of feasting on his flesh, making sandals of his hide, and selling the teeth to the Europeans, inspire every one with courage, and the animal seldom escapes from his pursuers; but in the plains of Bambarra and Kaarta, and the extensive wilds of Jallonkadoo, the elephants are very numerous, and, from the great scarcity of gunpowder in those districts, they are less annoyed by the natives.

Scattered teeth are frequently picked up in the woods, and travellers are very diligent in looking for them. It is a common practice with the elephant to thrust his teeth under the roots of such shrubs and bushes as grow in the more dry and elevated parts of the country, where the soil is shallow. These bushes he easily overturns, and feeds on the roots, which are in general more tender and juicy than the hard, woody branches or the foliage; but when the teeth are partly decayed by age, and the roots more firmly fixed, the great exertions of the animal in this practice frequently cause them to break short. At Kamalia I saw two teeth, one a very large one, which were found in the woods, and which were evidently broken off in this manner. Indeed, it is difficult otherwise to account for such a large proportion of broken ivory as is daily offered for sale at the different factories, for when the elephant is killed in hunting, unless he dashes himself over a precipice, the teeth are always extracted entire.

There are certain seasons of the year when the elephants collect into large herds, and traverse the country in quest of food or water; and as all that part of the country to the north of the Niger is destitute of rivers, whenever the pools in the woods are dried up the elephants approach towards the banks of that river. Here they continue until the commencement of the rainy season, in the months of June or July, and during this time they are much hunted by such of the Bambarrans as have gunpowder to spare. The elephant-hunters seldom go out singly—a party of four or five join together, and having each furnished himself with powder and ball, and a quantity of corn-meal in a leather bag sufficient for five or six days' provision, they enter the most unfrequented parts of the wood, and examine with great care everything that can lead to the discovery of the elephants. In this pursuit, notwithstanding the bulk of the animal, very great nicety of observation is required. The broken branches, the scattered dung of the animal, and the marks of his feet are carefully inspected; and many of the hunters have, by long experience and attentive observation, become so expert in their search that as soon as they observe the foot-marks of an elephant they will tell almost to a certainty at what time it passed and at what distance it will be found.

When they discover a herd of elephants, they follow them at a distance, until they perceive some one stray from the rest and come into such a situation as to be fired at with advantage. The hunters then approach with great caution, creeping amongst the long grass, until they have got near enough to be sure of their aim. They then discharge all their pieces at once, and throw themselves on their faces among the grass; the wounded elephant immediately applies his trunk to the different wounds, but being unable to extract the balls, and seeing nobody near him, he becomes quite furious and runs about amongst the bushes until by fatigue and loss of blood he has exhausted himself, and affords the hunters an opportunity of firing a second time at him, by which he is generally brought to the ground.

The skin is now taken off, and extended on the ground with pegs to dry; and such parts of the flesh as are most esteemed are cut up into thin slices, and dried in the sun, to serve for provisions on some future occasion. The teeth are struck out with a light hatchet which the hunters always carry along with them, not only for that purpose, but also to enable them to cut down such trees as contain honey; for though they carry with them only five or six days' provisions, they will remain in the woods for months if they are successful, and support themselves upon the flesh of such elephants as they kill and wild honey.

The ivory thus collected is seldom brought down to the coast by the hunters themselves. They dispose of it to the itinerant merchants who come annually from the coast with arms and ammunition to purchase this valuable commodity. Some of these merchants will collect ivory in the course of one season sufficient to load four or five asses. A great quantity of ivory is likewise brought from the interior by the slave coffles; there are, however, some slatees of the Mohammedan persuasion who, from motives of religion, will not deal in ivory, nor eat of the flesh of the elephant, unless it has been killed with a spear.

The quantity of ivory collected in this part of Africa is not so great, nor are the teeth in general so large, as in the countries nearer the Line: few of them weigh more than eighty or one hundred pounds, and upon an average a bar of European merchandise may be reckoned as the price of a pound of ivory.

I have now, I trust, in this and the preceding chapters explained with sufficient minuteness the nature and extent of the commercial connection which at present prevails, and has long subsisted, between the negro natives of those parts of Africa which I visited and the nations of Europe; and it appears that slaves, gold, and ivory, together with the few articles enumerated in the beginning of my work—viz., bees' wax and honey, hides, gums, and dye-woods—constitute the whole catalogue of exportable commodities. Other productions, however, have been incidentally noticed as the growth of Africa, such as grain of different kinds, tobacco, indigo, cotton-wool and perhaps a few others; but of all these (which can only be obtained by cultivation and labour) the natives raise sufficient only for their own immediate expenditure; nor, under the present system of their laws, manners, trade, and government, can anything further be expected from them. It cannot, however, admit of a doubt that all the rich and valuable productions both of the East and West Indies might easily be naturalised and brought to the utmost perfection in the tropical parts of this immense continent. Nothing is wanting to this end but example to enlighten the minds of the natives, and instruction to enable them to direct their industry to proper objects. It was not possible for me to behold the wonderful fertility of the soil, the vast herds of cattle, proper both for labour and food, and a variety of other circumstances favourable to colonisation and agriculture—and reflect, withal, on the means which presented themselves of a vast inland navigation without—lamenting that a country so abundantly gifted and favoured by nature should remain in its present savage and neglected state. Much more did I lament that a people of manners and disposition so gentle and benevolent should either be left as they now are, immersed in the gross and uncomfortable blindness of pagan superstition, or permitted to become converts to a system of bigotry and fanaticism which, without enlightening the mind, often debases the heart. On this subject many observations might be made, but the reader will probably think that I have already digressed too largely; and I now, therefore, return to my situation at Kamalia.

CHAPTER XXIV.
MOHAMMEDAN CUSTOMS;
ARRIVAL AT KINYTAKOORO.

The schoolmaster to whose care I was entrusted during the absence of Karfa was a man of a mild disposition and gentle manners; his name was Fankooma, and although he himself adhered strictly to the religion of Mohammed, he was by no means intolerant in his principles towards others who differed from him. He spent much of his time in reading, and teaching appeared to be his pleasure as well as employment. His school consisted of seventeen boys, most of whom were sons of Kafirs, and two girls, one of whom was Karfa's own daughter. The girls received their instruction in the daytime, but the boys always had their lessons, by the light of a large fire, before day break and again late in the evening; for, being considered, during their scholarship, as the domestic slaves of the master, they were employed in planting corn, bringing firewood, and in other servile offices through the day.

Exclusive of the Koran, and a book or two of commentaries thereon, the schoolmaster possessed a variety of manuscripts, which had partly been purchased from the trading Moors, and partly borrowed from bushreens in the neighbourhood and copied with great care. Other manuscripts had been produced to me at different places in the course of my journey; and on recounting those I had before seen, and those which were now shown to me, and interrogating the schoolmaster on the subject, I discovered that the negroes are in possession (among others) of an Arabic version of the Pentateuch of Moses, which they call *Taureta la Moosa*. This is so highly esteemed that it is often sold for the value of one prime slave. They have likewise a version of the Psalms of David (*Zabora Dawidi*); and, lastly, the Book of Isaiah, which they call *Lingeeli la Isa*, and it is in very high esteem. I suspect, indeed, that in all these copies there are interpolations of some of the peculiar tenets of Mohammed, for I could distinguish in many passages the name of the Prophet. It is possible, however, that this circumstance might otherwise have been accounted for if my knowledge of the Arabic had been more extensive. By means of those books many of the converted negroes have acquired an acquaintance with some of the remarkable events recorded in the

Old Testament. The account of our first parents, the death of Abel, the Deluge, the lives of Abraham, Isaac, and Jacob, the story of Joseph and his brethren, the history of Moses, David, Solomon, etc.; all these have been related to me, in the Mandingo language, with tolerable exactness by different people; and my surprise was not greater, on hearing these accounts from the lips of the negroes, than theirs on finding that I was already acquainted with them; for although the negroes in general have a very great idea of the wealth and power of the Europeans, I am afraid that the Mohammedan converts among them think but very lightly of our superior attainments in religious knowledge. The white traders in the maritime districts take no pains to counteract this unhappy prejudice, always performing their own devotions in secret, and seldom condescending to converse with the negroes in a friendly and instructive manner. To me, therefore, it was not so much the subject of wonder as matter of regret to observe that, while the superstition of Mohammed has in this manner scattered a few faint beams of learning among these poor people, the precious light of Christianity is altogether excluded. I could not but lament that, although the coast of Africa has now been known and frequented by the Europeans for more than two hundred years, yet the negroes still remain entire strangers to the doctrines of our holy religion. We are anxious to draw from obscurity the opinions and records of antiquity, the beauties of Arabian and Asiatic literature, etc.; but while our libraries are thus stored with the learning of various countries, we distribute with a parsimonious hand the blessings of religious truth to the benighted nations of the earth. The natives of Asia derive but little advantage in this respect from an intercourse with us; and even the poor Africans, whom we affect to consider as barbarians, look upon us, I fear, as little better than a race of formidable but ignorant heathens. When I produced Richardson's Arabic Grammar to some slatees on the Gambia, they were astonished to think that any European should understand and write the sacred language of their religion. At first they suspected that it might have been written by some of the slaves carried from the coast, but on a closer examination they were satisfied that no bushreen could write such beautiful Arabic, and one of them offered to give me an ass and sixteen bars of goods if I would part with the book. Perhaps a short and easy introduction to Christianity, such as is found in some of the catechisms for children, elegantly printed in Arabic, and distributed on different parts of the coast, might have a wonderful effect. The expense would be but trifling; curiosity would induce many to read it; and the evident superiority which it would possess over their present manuscripts, both in point of elegance and cheapness, might at last obtain it a place among the school-books of Africa.

The reflections which I have thus ventured to submit to my readers on this important subject naturally suggested themselves to my mind on perceiving the encouragement which was thus given to learning (such as it is) in many parts of Africa. I have observed that the pupils at Kamalia were most of them the children of pagans; their parents, therefore, could have had no predilection for the doctrines of Mohammed. Their aim was their children's improvement; and if a more enlightened system had presented itself, it would probably have been preferred. The children, too, wanted not a spirit of emulation, which it is the aim of the tutor to encourage. When any one of them has read through the Koran, and performed a certain number of public prayers, a feast is prepared by the schoolmaster, and the scholar undergoes an examination, or (in European terms) *takes out his degree*. I attended at three different inaugurations of this sort, and heard with pleasure the distinct and intelligent answers which the scholars frequently gave to the bushreens, who assembled on those occasions and acted as examiners. When the bushreens had satisfied themselves respecting the learning and abilities of the scholar, the last page of the Koran was put into his hand, and he was desired to read it aloud. After the boy had finished this lesson, he pressed the paper against his forehead and pronounced the word *Amen*, upon which all the bushreens rose, and, shaking him cordially by the hand, bestowed upon him the title of bushreen.

When a scholar has undergone this examination, his parents are informed that he has completed his education, and that it is incumbent on them to redeem their son by giving to the schoolmaster a slave or the price of a slave in exchange, which is always done if the parents can afford to do it; if not, the boy remains the domestic slave of the schoolmaster until he can, by his own industry, collect goods sufficient to ransom himself.

About a week after the departure of Karfa three Moors arrived at Kamalia with a considerable quantity of salt and other merchandise, which they had obtained on credit from a merchant of Fezzan, who had lately arrived at Kancaba. Their engagement was to pay him his price when the goods were sold, which they expected would be in the course of a month. Being rigid bushreens, they were accommodated with two of Karfa's huts, and sold their goods to very great advantage.

On the 24th of January Karfa returned to Kamalia with a number of people and thirteen prime slaves whom he had purchased. He likewise brought with him a young girl whom he had married at Kancaba, as his fourth wife, and had given her parents three prime slaves for her. She was kindly received at the door of the baloon by Karfa's other wives, who conducted their new acquaintance and co-partner into one of the best huts, which they had caused to be swept and whitewashed on purpose to receive her.

My clothes were by this time become so very ragged that I was almost ashamed to appear out of doors, but Karfa, on the day after his arrival, generously presented me with such a garment and trousers as are commonly worn in the country.

The slaves which Karfa had brought with him were all of them prisoners of war; they had been taken by the Bambarra army in the kingdoms of Wassela and Kaarta, and carried to Sego, where some of them had remained three years in irons. From Sego they were sent, in company with a number of other captives, up the Niger in two large canoes, and offered for sale at Yamina, Bammakoo, and Kancaba; at which places the greater number of the captives were bartered for gold dust, and the remainder sent forward to Kankaree.

Eleven of them confessed to me that they had been slaves from their infancy, but the other two refused to give any account of their former condition. They were all very inquisitive, but they viewed me at first with looks of horror, and repeatedly asked if my countrymen were cannibals. They were very desirous to know what became of the slaves after they had crossed the salt water. I told them that they were employed in cultivation the land; but they would not believe me, and one of them, putting his hand upon the ground, said, with great simplicity, "Have you really got such ground as this to set your feet upon?" A deeply-rooted idea that the whites purchase negroes for the purpose of devouring them, or of selling them to others that they may be devoured hereafter, naturally makes the slaves contemplate a journey towards the coast with great terror, insomuch that the slatees are forced to keep them constantly in irons, and watch them very closely, to prevent their escape. They are commonly secured by putting the right leg of one and the left of another into the same pair of fetters. By supporting the fetters with a string, they can walk, though very slowly. Every four slaves are likewise fastened together by the necks with a strong rope of twisted thongs, and in the night an additional pair of fetters is put on their hands, and sometimes a light iron chain passed round their necks.

Such of them as evince marks of discontent are secured in a different manner. A thick billet of wood is cut about three feet long, and, a smooth notch being made upon one side of it, the ankle of the slave is bolted to the smooth part by means of a strong iron staple, one prong of which passes on each side of the ankle. All these fetters and bolts are made from native iron; in the present case they were put on by the blacksmith as soon as the slaves arrived from Kancaba, and were not taken off until the morning on which the coffle departed for Gambia.

In other respects the treatment of the slaves during their stay at Kamalia was far from being harsh or cruel. They were led out in their fetters every morning to the shade of the tamarind-tree, where they were encouraged to play at games of hazard, and sing diverting songs, to keep up their spirits; for, though some of them sustained the hardships of their situation with amazing fortitude, the greater part were very much dejected, and would sit all day in a sort of sullen melancholy, with their eyes fixed upon the ground. In the evening their irons were examined, and their hand-fetters put on, after which they were conducted into two large huts, where they were guarded during the night by Karfa's domestic slaves. But, notwithstanding all this, about a week after their arrival, one of the slaves had the address to procure a small knife, with which he opened the rings of his fetters, cut the rope, and made his escape; more of them would probably have got off had they assisted each other, but the slave no sooner found himself at liberty than he refused to stop and assist in breaking the chain which was fastened round the necks of his companions.

As all the slatees and slaves belonging to the coffle were now assembled either at Kamalia or at some of the neighbouring villages, it might have been expected that we should set out immediately for Gambia; but though the day of our departure was frequently fixed, it was always found expedient to change it. Some of the people had not prepared their dry provisions; others had gone to visit their relations; or collect some trifling debts; and, last of all, it was necessary to consult whether the day would be a lucky one. On account of one of these, or other such causes, our departure was put off, day after day, until the month of February was far advanced, after which all the slatees agreed to remain in their present quarters until the *fast moon was over*. And here I may remark that loss of time is an object of no great importance in the eyes of a negro. If he has anything of consequence to perform, it is a matter of indifference to him whether he does it to-day or to-morrow, or a month or two hence; so long as he can spend the present moment with any degree of comfort, he gives himself very little concern about the future.

The fast of Ramadan was observed with great strictness by all the bushreens, but instead of compelling me to follow their example, as the Moors did on a similar occasion, Karfa frankly told me that I was at liberty to pursue my own inclination. In order, however, to manifest a respect for their religious opinions, I voluntarily fasted three days, which was thought sufficient to screen me from the reproachful epithet of kafir. During the fast all the slatees belonging to the coffle assembled every morning in Karfa's house, where the schoolmaster read to them some religious lessons from a large folio volume, the author of which was an Arab of the name of Sheiffa. In the evening such of the women as had embraced Mohammedanism assembled and said their prayers publicly at the missura. They were all dressed in white, and went through the different prostrations prescribed by their religion with becoming solemnity. Indeed, during the whole fast of Ramadan the negroes behaved themselves with the greatest meekness and humility, forming a striking contrast to the savage intolerance and brutal bigotry which at this period characterise the Moors.

When the fast month was almost at an end, the bushreens assembled at the missura to watch for the appearance of the new moon, but, the evening being rather cloudy, they were for some time disappointed, and a number of them had gone home with a resolution to fast another day, when on a sudden this delightful object showed her sharp horns from behind a cloud, and was welcomed with the clapping of hands, beating of drums, firing of muskets, and other marks of rejoicing. As this moon is reckoned extremely lucky, Karfa gave orders that all the people belonging to the coffle should immediately pack up their dry provisions and hold themselves in readiness; and on the 16th of April the slatees held a consultation and fixed on the 19th of the same month as the day on which the coffle should depart from Kamalia. This resolution freed me from much uneasiness, for our departure had already been so long deferred that I was apprehensive it might still be put off until the commencement of the rainy season; and although Karfa behaved towards me with the greatest kindness, I found my situation very unpleasant. The slatees were unfriendly to me, and the trading Moors who were at this time at Kamalia continued to plot mischief against me from the first day of their arrival. Under these circumstances I reflected that my life in a great measure depended on the good opinion of an individual who was daily hearing malicious stories concerning the Europeans, and I could hardly expect that he would always judge with impartiality between me and his countrymen. Time had, indeed, reconciled me in some degree to their mode of life, and a smoky hut or a scanty supper gave me no great uneasiness; but I became at last wearied out with a constant state of alarm and anxiety, and felt a painful longing for the manifold blessings of civilised society.

April 19.—The long-wished-for day of our departure was at length arrived; and the slatees, having taken the irons from their slaves, assembled with them at the door of Karfa's house, where the bundles were all tied up, and every one had his load assigned him. The coffle, on its departure from Kamalia, consisted of twenty-seven slaves for sale, the property of Karfa and four other slatees; but we were afterwards joined by five at Maraboo and three at Bala—making in all thirty-five slaves. The freemen were fourteen in number, but most of them had one or two wives and some domestic slaves; and the schoolmaster, who was now upon his return for Woradoo, the place of his nativity, took with him eight of his scholars, so that the number of free people and domestic slaves amounted to thirty-eight, and the whole amount of the coffle was seventy-three. Among the freemen were six jillikeas (singing men), whose musical talents were frequently exerted either to divert our fatigue or obtain us a welcome from strangers. When we departed from Kamalia, we were followed for about half a mile by most of the inhabitants of the town, some of them crying and others shaking hands with their relations who were now about to leave them; and when we had gained a piece of rising ground, from which we had a view of Kamalia, all the people belonging to the coffle were ordered to sit down in one place with their faces towards the west, and the townspeople were desired to sit down in another place with their faces towards Kamalia. In this situation the schoolmaster, with two of the principal slatees, having taken their places between the two parties, pronounced a long and solemn prayer, after which they walked three times round the coffle, making an impression in the ground with the ends of their spears, and muttering something by way of charm. When this ceremony was ended, all the people belonging to the coffle sprang up and, without taking a formal farewell of their friends, set forwards. As many of the slaves had remained for years in irons, the sudden exertion of walking quick with heavy loads upon their heads occasioned spasmodic contractions of their legs; and we had not proceeded above a mile before it was found necessary to take two of them from the rope, and allow them to walk more slowly until we reached Maraboo, a walled village, where some people were waiting to join the coffle. Here we stopped about two hours, to allow the strangers time to pack up their provisions, and then continued our route to Bala, which town we reached about four in the afternoon. The inhabitants of Bala at this season of the year subsist chiefly on fish, which they take in great plenty from the streams in the neighbourhood. We remained here until the afternoon of the next day, the 20th, when we proceeded to Worumbang, the frontier village of Manding, towards Jallonkadoo. As we proposed shortly to enter the Jallonka Wilderness, the people of this village furnished us with great plenty of provisions, and on the morning of the 21st we entered the woods to the westward of Worumbang. After having travelled some little way, a consultation was held whether we should continue our route through the wilderness, or save one day's provisions by going to Kinytakooro, a town in Jallonkadoo. After debating the matter for some time, it was agreed that we should take the road for Kinytakooro; but as that town was a long day's journey distant, it was necessary to take some refreshment. Accordingly every person opened his provision-bag and brought a handful or two of meal to the place where Karfa and the slatees were sitting. When every one had brought his quota, and the whole was properly arranged in small gourd-shells, the schoolmaster offered up a short prayer, the substance of which was that God and the holy Prophet might preserve us from robbers and all bad people, that our provisions might never fail us, nor our limbs become fatigued. This ceremony being ended, every one partook of the meal and drank a little water, after which we set forward (rather running than walking) until we came to the river Kokoro, a branch of the Senegal, where we halted about ten minutes. The banks of this river are very high, and from the grass and brushwood which had been left by the stream it was evident that at this place the water had risen more than twenty feet perpendicular during the rainy season. At this time it was only a small stream, such as would turn a mill, swarming with fish; and on account of the number of crocodiles, and the danger of being carried past the ford by the force of the stream in the rainy season, it is called *Kokoro* (dangerous). From this place we continued to travel with the greatest expedition, and in the afternoon crossed two small branches of the Kokoro. About sunset we came in sight of Kinytakooro, a considerable town, nearly square, situated in the middle of a large and well-cultivated plain: before we entered the town, we halted until the people who had fallen behind came up. During this day's travel two slaves, a woman and a girl, belonging to a slatee of Bala, were so much fatigued that they could not keep up with the coffle; they were severely whipped, and dragged along until about three o'clock in the afternoon, when they were both affected with vomiting, by which it was discovered that they had *eaten* clay. This practice is by no means uncommon amongst the negroes; but whether it arises from a vitiated appetite, or from a settled intention to destroy themselves, I cannot affirm. They were permitted to lie down in the woods, and three people remained with them until they had rested themselves; but they did not arrive at the town until past midnight, and were then so much exhausted that the slatee gave up all thoughts of taking them across the woods in their present condition, and determined to return with them to Bala and wait for another opportunity.

As this was the first town beyond the limits of Manding, greater etiquette than usual was observed. Every person was ordered to keep in his proper station, and we marched towards the town in a sort of procession nearly as follows:—In front five or six singing men, all of them belonging to the coffle; these were followed by the other free people; then came the slaves, fastened in the usual way by a rope round their necks, four of them to a rope, and a man with a spear between each four; after them came the domestic slaves; and in the rear the women of free condition, wives of the slatees, etc. In this manner we proceeded until we came within a hundred yards of the gate, when the singing men began a loud song, well calculated to flatter the vanity of the inhabitants, by extolling their known hospitality to strangers and their particular friendship for the Mandingoes. When we entered the town we proceeded to the bentang, where the people gathered round us to hear our *dentegi* (history); this was related publicly by two of the singing men— they enumerated every little circumstance which had happened to the coffle, beginning with the events of the present day and relating everything in a backward series until they reached Kamalia. When this history was ended, the master of the town gave them a small present, and all the people of the coffle, both free and enslaved, were invited by some person or other and accommodated with lodging and provisions for the night.

CHAPTER XXV.
THE JALLONKA WILDERNESS; A WARLIKE TALE.

We continued at Kinytakooro until noon of the 22nd of April, when we removed to a village about seven miles to the westward, the inhabitants of which, being apprehensive of hostilities from the Foulahs of Fooladoo, were at this time employed in constructing small temporary huts among the rocks, on the side of a high hill close to the village. The situation was almost impregnable, being everywhere surrounded with high precipices, except on the eastern side, where the natives had left a pathway sufficient to allow one person at a time to ascend. Upon the brow of the hill, immediately over this path, I observed several heaps of large loose stones, which the people told me were intended to be thrown down upon the Foulahs if they should attempt the hill.

At daybreak on the 23rd we departed from this village and entered the Jallonka Wilderness. We passed in the course of the morning the ruins of two small towns which had lately been burnt by the Foulahs. The fire must have been very intense, for I observed that the walls of many of the huts were slightly vitrified, and appeared at a distance as if covered with a red varnish. About ten o'clock we came to the river Wonda, which is somewhat larger than the river Kokoro; but the stream was at this the rather muddy, which Karfa assured me was occasioned by amazing shoals of fish. They were indeed seen in all directions, and in such abundance that I fancied the water itself tasted and smelt fishy. As soon as we had crossed the river, Karfa gave orders that all the people of the coffle should in future keep close together, and travel in their proper station. The guides and young men were accordingly placed in the van, the women and slaves in the centre, and the freemen in the rear. In this order we travelled with uncommon expedition through a woody but beautiful country, interspersed with a pleasing variety of hill and dale, and abounding with partridges, guinea-fowl, and deer, until sunset, when we arrived at a most romantic stream, called Co-meissang. My arms and neck having been exposed to the sun during the whole day, and irritated by the rubbing of my dress in walking, were now very much inflamed and covered with blisters, and I was happy to embrace the opportunity, while the coffle rested on the bank of the river, to bathe myself in the stream. This practice, together with the cool of the evening, much diminished the inflammation. About three miles to the westward of the Co-meissang we halted in a thick wood and kindled our fires for the night. We were all by this time very much fatigued, having, as I judged, travelled this day thirty miles, but no person was heard to complain. Whilst supper was preparing, Karfa made one of the slaves break some branches from the trees for my bed. When we had finished our supper of kouskous, moistened with some boiling water, and put the slaves in irons, we all lay down to sleep; but we were frequently disturbed in the night by the howling of wild beasts, and we found the small brown ants very troublesome.

April 24.—Before daybreak the bushreens said their morning prayers, and most of the free people drank a little *moening* (a sort of gruel), part of which was likewise given to such of the slaves as appeared least able to sustain the fatigues of the day. One of Karfa's female slaves was very sulky, and when some gruel was offered to her she refused to drink it. As soon as day dawned we set out, and travelled the whole morning over a wild and rocky country, by which my feet were much bruised, and I was sadly apprehensive that I should not he able to keep up with the coffle during the day; but I was in a great measure relieved from this anxiety when I observed that others were more exhausted than myself. In particular, the woman slave who had refused victuals in the morning began now to lag behind, and complain dreadfully of pains in her legs. Her load was taken from her and given to another slave, and she was ordered to keep in the front of the coffle. About eleven o'clock, as we were resting by a small rivulet, some of the people discovered a hive of bees in a hollow tree, and they were proceeding to obtain the honey when the largest swarm I ever beheld flew out, and, attacking the people of the coffle, made us fly in all directions. I took the alarm first, and, I believe, was the only person who escaped with impunity. When our enemies thought fit to desist from pursuing us, and every person was employed in picking out the stings he had received, it was discovered that the poor woman above mentioned, whose name was Nealee, was not come up; and as many of the slaves in their retreat had left their brindles behind them, it became necessary for some persons to return and bring them. In order to do this with safety, fire was set to the grass a considerable way to the eastward of the hive, and, the wind driving the fire furiously along, the party pushed through the smoke and recovered the bundles. They likewise brought with them poor Nealee, whom they found lying by the rivulet. She was very much exhausted, and had crept to the stream in hopes to defend herself from the bees by throwing water over her body; but this proved ineffectual, for she was stung in the most dreadful manner.

When the slatees had picked out the stings as far as they could, she was washed with water and then rubbed with bruised leaves; but the wretched woman obstinately refused to proceed any farther, declaring that she would rather die than walk another step. As entreaties and threats were used in vain, the whip was at length applied; and after bearing patiently a few strokes she started up and walked with tolerable expedition for four or five hours longer, when she made an attempt to run away from the coffle, but was so very weak that she fell down in the grass. Though she was unable to rise, the whip was a second time applied, but without effect; upon which Karfa desired two of the slatees to place her upon the ass which carried our dry provisions; but she could not sit erect, and the ass being very refractory it was found impossible to carry her forward in that manner. The slatees, however, were unwilling to abandon her, the day's journey being nearly ended; they therefore made a sort of litter of bamboo-canes, upon which she was placed, and tied on it with slips of bark. This litter was carried upon the heads of two slaves, one walking before the other, and they were followed by two others, who relieved them occasionally. In this manner the woman was carried forward until it was dark, when we reached a stream of water at the foot of a high hill called Gankaran-Kooro, and here we stopped for the night, and set about preparing our supper. As we had only ate one handful of meal since the preceding night, and travelled all day in a hot sun, many of the slaves who had loads upon their heads were very much fatigued, and some of them *snapped their fingers*, which among the negroes is a sure sign of desperation. The slatees immediately put them all in irons, and such of them as had evinced signs of great despondency were kept apart from the rest, and had their hands tied. In the morning they were found greatly recovered.

April 25.—At daybreak poor Nealee was awakened, but her limbs were now become so stiff and painful that she could neither walk nor stand; she was therefore lifted, like a corpse, upon the back of the ass, and the slatees endeavoured to secure her in that situation by fastening her hands together under the ass's neck, and her feet under the belly, with long slips of bark; but the ass was so very unruly that no sort of treatment could induce him to proceed with his load, and as Nealee made no exertion to prevent herself from falling she was quickly thrown off, and had one of her legs much bruised. Every attempt to carry her forward being thus found ineffectual, the general cry of the coffle was *Kang-tegi, kang-tegi* ("Cut her throat, cut her throat")—an operation I did not wish to see performed, and therefore marched onwards with the foremost of the coffle. I had not walked above a mile, when one of Karfa's domestic slaves came up to me, with poor Nealea's garment upon the end of his bow, and exclaimed, *Nealee affeeleeta* ("Nealee is lost")! I asked him whether the slatees had given him the garment as a reward for cutting her throat. He replied that Karfa and the schoolmaster would not consent to that measure, but had left her on the road, where undoubtedly she soon perished, and was probably devoured by wild beasts.

The sad fate of this wretched woman, notwithstanding the outcry before mentioned, made a strong impression on the mind of the whole coffle, and the schoolmaster fasted the whole of the ensuing day in consequence of it. We proceeded in deep silence, and soon afterwards crossed the river Furkoomah, which was about as large as the river Wonda. We now travelled with great expedition, every one being apprehensive he might otherwise meet with the fate of poor Nealee. It was, however, with great difficulty that I could keep up, although I threw away my spear and everything that could in the least obstruct me. About noon we saw a large herd of elephants, but they suffered us to pass unmolested; and in the evening we halted near a thicket of bamboo, but found no water, so that we were forced to proceed four miles farther to a small stream, where we stopped for the night. We had marched this day, as I judged, about twenty-six miles.

April 26.—This morning two of the schoolmaster's pupils complained much of pains in their legs, and one of the slaves walked lame, the soles of his feet being very much blistered and inflamed; we proceeded, notwithstanding, and about eleven o'clock began to ascend a rocky hill called Boki-Kooro, and it was past two in the afternoon before we reached the level ground on the other side. This was the most rocky road we had yet encountered, and it hurt our feet much. In a short time we arrived at a pretty large river, called Boki, which we forded; it ran smooth and clear over a bed of whinstone. About a mile to the westward of the river we came to a road which leads to the northeast towards Gadou, and seeing the marks of many horses' feet upon the soft sand, the slatees conjectured that a party of plunderers had lately rode that way to fall upon some town of Gadou; and lest they should discover upon their return that we had passed, and attempt to pursue us by the marks of our feet, the coffle was ordered to disperse and travel in a loose manner through the high grass and bushes. A little before it was dark, having crossed the ridge of hills to the westward of the river Boki, we came to a well called *Cullong Qui* (White Sand Well), and here we rested for the night.

April 27.—We departed from the well early in the morning, and walked on with the greatest alacrity, in hopes of reaching a town before night. The road during the forenoon led through extensive thickets of dry bamboos. About two o'clock we came to a stream called Nunkolo, where we were each of us regaled with a handful of meal, which, according to a superstitious custom, was not to be eaten until it was first moistened with water from this stream. About four o'clock we reached Sooseeta, a small Jallonka village, situated in the district of Kullo, which comprehends all that tract of country lying along the banks of the Black River, or main branch of the Senegal. These were the first human habitations we had seen since we left the village to the westward of Kinytakooro, having travelled in the course of the last five days upwards of one hundred miles. Here, after a great deal of entreaty, we were provided with huts to sleep in, but the master of the village plainly told us that he could not give us any provisions, as there had lately been a great scarcity in this part of the country. He assured us that, before they had gathered in their present crops, the whole inhabitants of Kullo had been for twenty-nine days without tasting corn, during which time they supported themselves entirely upon the yellow powder which is found in the pods of the *nitta*, so called by the natives, a species of mimosa, and upon the seeds of the bamboo-cane, which, when properly pounded and dressed, taste very much like rice. As our dry provisions were not yet exhausted, a considerable quantity of kouskous was dressed for supper, and many of the villagers were invited to take part of the repast; but they made a very bad return for this kindness, for in the night they seized upon one of the schoolmaster's boys, who had fallen asleep under the bentang tree, and carried him away. The boy fortunately awoke before he was far from the village, and, setting up a loud scream, the man who carried him put his hand upon his mouth and ran with him into the woods; but afterwards understanding that he belonged to the schoolmaster, whose place of residence is only three days' journey distant, he thought, I suppose, that he could not retain him as a slave without the schoolmaster's knowledge, and therefore stripped off the boy's clothes and permitted him to return.

April 28.—Early in the morning we departed from Sooseeta, and about ten o'clock came to an unwalled town, called Manna, the inhabitants of which were employed in collecting the fruit of the nitta-trees, which are very numerous in this neighbourhood. The pods are long and narrow, and contain a few black seeds, enveloped in the fine mealy powder before mentioned; the meal itself is of a bright yellow colour, resembling the flour of sulphur, and has a sweet mucilaginous taste. When eaten by itself it is clammy, but when mixed with milk or water it constitutes a very pleasant and nourishing article of diet.

The language of the people of Manna is the same that is spoken all over that extensive and hilly country called Jallonkadoo. Some of the words have a great affinity to the Mandingo, but the natives themselves consider it as a distinct language. Their numerals are these:—

One	Kidding.
Two	Fidding.
Three	Sarra.

Four	Nani.
Five	Soolo.
Six	Seni.
Seven	Soolo ma fidding.
Eight	Soolo ma sarra.
Nine	Soolo ma nani.
Ten	Nuff.

The Jallonkas, like the Mandingoes, are governed by a number of petty chiefs, who are in a great measure independent of each other. They have no common sovereign, and the chiefs are seldom upon such terms of friendship as to assist each other even in war-time. The chief of Manna, with a number of his people, accompanied us to the banks of the Bafing, or Black River (a principal branch of the Senegal), which we crossed upon a bridge of bamboos of a very singular construction. The river at this place is smooth and deep, and has very little current. Two tall trees, when tied together by the tops, are sufficiently long to reach from one side to the other, the roots resting upon the rocks, and the tops floating in the water. When a few trees have been placed in this direction, they are covered with dry bamboos, so as to form a floating bridge, with a sloping gangway at each end, where the trees rest upon the rocks. This bridge is carried away every year by the swelling of the river in the rainy season, and is constantly rebuilt by the inhabitants of Manna, who, on that account, expect a small tribute from every passenger.

In the afternoon we passed several villages, at none of which we could procure a lodging, and in the twilight we received information that two hundred Jallonkas had assembled near a town called Melo, with a view to plunder the coffle. This induced us to alter our course, and we travelled with great secrecy until midnight, when we approached a town called Koba. Before we entered the town the names of all the people belonging to the coffle were called over, and a freeman and three slaves were found to be missing. Every person immediately concluded that the slaves had murdered the freeman and made their escape. It was therefore agreed that six people should go back as far as the last village, and endeavour to find his body, or collect some information concerning the slaves. In the meantime the coffle was ordered to lie concealed in a cotton-field near a large nitta-tree, and nobody to speak except in a whisper. It was towards morning before the six men returned, having heard nothing of the man or the slaves. As none of us had tasted victuals for the last twenty-four hours, it was agreed that we should go into Koba and endeavour to procure some provisions. We accordingly entered the town before it was quite day, and Karfa purchased from the chief man, for three strings of beads, a considerable quantity of ground nuts, which we roasted and ate for breakfast. We were afterwards provided with huts, and rested here for the day.

About eleven o'clock, to our great joy and surprise, the freeman and slaves who had parted from the coffle the preceding night entered the town. One of the slaves, it seems, had hurt his foot, and the night being very dark they soon lost sight of the coffle. The freeman, as soon as he found himself alone with the slaves was aware of his own danger, and insisted on putting them in irons. The slaves were at first rather unwilling to submit, but when he threatened to stab them one by one with his spear, they made no farther resistance; and he remained with them among the bushes until morning, when he let them out of irons, and came to the town in hopes of hearing which route the coffle had taken. The information that we received concerning the Jallonkas who intended to rob the coffle was this day confirmed, and we were forced to remain here until the afternoon of the 30th, when Karfa hired a number of people to protect us, and we proceeded to a village called Tinkingtang. Departing from this village on the day following, we crossed a high ridge of mountains to the west of the Black River, and travelled over a rough stony country until sunset, when we arrived at Lingicotta, a small village in the district of Woradoo. Here we shook out the last handful of meal from our dry provision-bags, this being the second day, since we crossed the Black River, that we had travelled from morning until night without tasting one morsel of food.

May 2.—We departed from Lingicotta; but the slaves being very much fatigued, we halted for the night at a village about nine miles to the westward, and procured some provisions through the interest of the schoolmaster, who now sent forward a messenger to Malacotta, his native town, to inform his friends of his arrival in the country, and to desire them to provide the necessary quantity of victuals to entertain the coffle for two or three days.

May 3.—We set out for Malacotta, and about noon arrived at a village near a considerable stream of water which flows to the westward. Here we determined to stop for the return of the messenger who had been sent to Malacotta the day before; and as the natives assured me there were no crocodiles in this stream, I went and bathed myself. Very few people here can swim, for they came in numbers to dissuade me from venturing into a pool where they said the water would come over my head. About two o'clock the messenger returned from Malacotta, and the schoolmaster's elder brother, being impatient to see him, came along with the messenger to meet him at this village. The interview between the two brothers, who had not seen each other for nine years, was very natural and affecting. They fell upon each other's neck, and it was some time before either of them could speak. At length, when the schoolmaster had a little recovered himself, he took his brother by the hand, and turning round, "This is the man," said he, pointing to Karfa, "who has been my father in Manding. I would have pointed him out sooner to you, but my heart was too full."

We reached Malacotta in the evening, where we were well received. This is an unwalled town. The huts for the most part are made of split cane, twisted into a sort of wicker-work, and plastered over with mud. Here we remained three days, and were each day presented with a bullock from the schoolmaster. We were likewise well entertained by the townspeople, who appear to be very active and industrious. They make very good soap by boiling ground nuts in water, and then adding a ley of wood-ashes. They likewise manufacture excellent iron, which they carry to Bondou to barter for salt. A party of the townspeople had lately returned from a trading expedition of this kind, and brought information concerning a war between Almami Abdulkader, king of Foota-Torra, and Damel, king of the Jaloffs. The events of this war soon became a favourite subject with the singing men and the common topic of conversation in all the kingdoms bordering upon the Senegal and Gambia; and, as the account is somewhat singular, I shall here abridge it for the reader's information. The king of Foota-Torra, inflamed with a zeal for propagating his religion, had sent an embassy to Damel similar to that which he had sent to Kasson, as has been previously related. The ambassador on the present occasion was accompanied by two of the principal bushreens, who carried each a large knife fixed on the top of a long pole. As soon as he had procured admission into the presence of Damel, and announced the pleasure of his Sovereign, he ordered the bushreens to present the emblems of his mission. The two knives were accordingly laid before Damel, and the ambassador explained himself as follows:—"With this knife," said he, "Abdulkader will condescend to shave the head of Damel, if Damel will embrace the Mohammedan faith; and with this other knife Abdulkader will cut the throat of Damel if Damel refuses to embrace it: take your choice." Damel coolly told the ambassador that he had no choice to make; he neither chose to have his head shaved nor his throat cut; and with this answer the ambassador was civilly dismissed. Abdulkader took his measures accordingly, and with a powerful army invaded Damel's country. The inhabitants of the towns and villages filled up their wells, destroyed their provisions, carried off their effects, and abandoned their dwellings as he approached. By this means he was led on from place to place, until he had advanced three days' journey into the country of the Jaloffs. He had, indeed, met with no opposition, but his army had suffered so much from the scarcity of water that several of his men had died by the way. This induced him to direct his march towards a watering-place in the woods, where his men, having quenched their thirst and being overcome with fatigue, lay down carelessly to sleep among the bushes. In this situation they were attacked by Damel before daybreak and completely routed. Many of them were trampled to death as they lay asleep by the Jaloff horses; others were killed in attempting to make their escape; and a still greater number were taken prisoners. Among the latter was Abdulkader himself. This ambitious, or, rather, frantic prince, who but a month before had sent the threatening message to Damel, was now himself led into his presence as a miserable captive. The behaviour of Damel on this occasion is never mentioned by the singing men but in terms of the highest approbation; and it was indeed so extraordinary in an African prince that the reader may find it difficult to give credit to the recital. When his royal prisoner was brought before him in irons, and thrown upon the ground, the magnanimous Damel, instead of setting his foot upon his neck and stabbing him with his spear, according to custom in such cases, addressed him as follows:—"Abdulkader, answer me this question. If the chance of war had placed me in your situation, and you in mine, how would you have treated me?" "I would have thrust my spear into your heart," returned Abdulkader, with great firmness; "and I know that a similar fate awaits me." "Not so," said Damel; "my spear is indeed red with the blood of your subjects, killed in battle, and I could now give it a deeper stain by dipping it in your own; but this would not build up my towns, nor bring to life the thousands who fell in the woods. I will not, therefore, kill you in cold blood, but I will retain you as my slave, until I perceive that your presence in your own kingdom will be no longer dangerous to your neighbours, and then I will consider of the proper way of disposing of you." Abdulkader was accordingly retained, and worked as a slave for three months; at the end of which period Damel listened to the solicitations of the inhabitants of Foota-Torra, and restored to them their king. Strange as this story may appear, I have no doubt of the truth of it. It was told me at Malacotta by the negroes; it was afterwards related to me by the Europeans on the Gambia, by some of the French at Goree, and confirmed by nine slaves who were taken prisoners along with Abdulkader by the watering-place in the woods and carried in the same ship with me to the West Indies.

CHAPTER XXVI.
MEETING WITH DR. LAIDLEY—RETURN TO THE COAST—VOYAGE TO ENGLAND.

On the 7th of May we departed from Malacotta, and having crossed the *Ba Lee* (Honey River), a branch of the Senegal, we arrived in the evening at a walled town called Bintingala, where we rested two days. From thence, in one day more, we proceeded to Dindikoo, a small town situated at the bottom of a high ridge of hills, from which this district is named *Konkodoo* (the country of mountains). These hills are very productive of gold. I was shown a small quantity of this metal which had been lately collected: the grains were about the usual size, but much flatter than those of Manding, and were found in white quartz, which had been broken to pieces by hammers. At this town I met with a negro whose hair and skin were of a dull white colour. He was of that sort which are called in the Spanish West Indies *albinos*, or white negroes. The skin is cadaverous and unsightly, and the natives considered this complexion (I believe truly) as the effect of disease.

May 11.—At daybreak we departed from Dindikoo, and, after a toilsome day's travel, arrived in the evening at Satadoo, the capital of a district of the same name. This town was formerly of considerable extent, but many families had left it in consequence of the predatory incursions of the Foulahs of Foota-Jalla, who made it a practice to come secretly through the woods and carry off people from the cornfields and even from the wells near the town. In the afternoon of the 12th we crossed the Falemé River, the same which I had formerly crossed at Bondou in my journey eastward. This river, at this season of the year, is easily forded at this place, the stream being only about two feet deep. The water is very pure, and flows rapidly over a bed of sand and gravel. We lodged for the night at a small village called Medina, the sole property of a Mandingo merchant who, by a long intercourse with Europeans, has been induced to adopt some of their customs. His victuals were served up in pewter dishes, and even his houses were built after the fashion of the English houses on the Gambia.

May 13.—In the morning, as we were preparing to depart, a coffle of slaves belonging to some Serawoolli traders crossed the river, and agreed to proceed with us to Baniserile, the capital of Dentila—a very long day's journey from this place. We accordingly set out together, and travelled with great expedition through the woods until noon, when one of the Serawoolli slaves dropped the load from his head, for which he was smartly whipped. The load was replaced, but he had not proceeded above a mile before he let it fall a second time, for which he received the same punishment. After this he travelled in great pain until about two o'clock, when we stopped to breathe a little by a pool of water, the day being remarkably hot. The poor slave was now so completely exhausted that his master was obliged to release him from the rope, for he lay motionless on the ground. A Serawoolli, therefore, undertook to remain with him and endeavour to bring him to the town during the cool of the night; in the meanwhile we continued our route, and after a very hard day's travel, arrived at Baniserile late in the evening.

One of our slatees was a native of this place, from which he had been absent three years. This man invited me to go with him to his house, at the gate of which his friends met him with many expressions of joy, shaking hands with him, embracing him, and singing and dancing before him. As soon as he had seated himself upon a mat by the threshold of his door, a young woman (his intended bride) brought a little water in a calabash, and, kneeling down before him, desired him to wash his hands; when he had done this the girl, with a tear of joy sparkling in her eyes, drank the water—this being considered as the greatest proof she could possibly give him of her fidelity and attachment. About eight o'clock the same evening the Serawoolli who had been left in the woods to take care of the fatigued slave returned and told us that he was dead; the general opinion, however, was that he himself had killed him or left him to perish on the road, for the Serawoollies are said to be infinitely more cruel in their treatment of slaves than the Mandingoes. We remained at Baniserile two days, in order to purchase native iron, shea-butter, and some other articles for sale on the Gambia; and here the slatee who had invited me to his house, and who possessed three slaves, part of the coffle, having obtained information that the price on the coast was very low, determined to separate from us and remain with his slaves where he was until an opportunity should offer of disposing of them to advantage—giving us to understand that he should complete his nuptials with the young woman before mentioned in the meantime.

May 16.—We departed from Baniserile and travelled through thick woods until noon, when we saw at a distance the town of Julifunda, but did not approach it, as we proposed to rest for the night at a large town called Kirwani, which we reached about four o'clock in the afternoon. This town stands in a valley, and the country for more than a mile round it is cleared of wood and well cultivated. The inhabitants appear to be very active and industrious, and seem to have carried the system of agriculture to some degree of perfection, for they collect the dung of their cattle into large heaps during the dry season for the purpose of manuring their land with it at the proper time. I saw nothing like this in any other part of Africa. Near the town are several smelting furnaces, from which the natives obtain very good iron. They afterwards hammer the metal into small bars, about a foot in length and two inches in breadth, one of which bars is sufficient to make two Mandingo corn-hoes. On the morning after our arrival we were visited by a slatee of this place, who informed Karfa that among some slaves he had lately purchased was a native of Foota-Jalla, and as that country was at no great distance he could not safely employ him in the labours of the field, lest he should effect his escape. The slatee was therefore desirous of exchanging this slave for one of Karfa's, and offered some cloth and shea-butter to induce Karfa to comply with the proposal, which was accepted. The slatee thereupon sent a boy to order the slave in question to bring him a few ground-nuts. The poor creature soon afterwards entered the court in which we were sitting, having no suspicion of what was negotiating, until the master caused the gate to be shut, and told him to sit down. The slave now saw his danger, and, perceiving the gate to be shut upon him, threw down the nuts and jumped over the fence. He was immediately pursued and overtaken by the slatees, who brought him back and secured him in irons, after which one of Karfa's slaves was released and delivered in exchange. The unfortunate captive was at first very much dejected, but in the course of a few days his melancholy gradually subsided, and he became at length as cheerful as any of his companions.

Departing from Kirwani on the morning of the 20th we entered the Tenda Wilderness, of two days' journey. The woods were very thick, and the country shelved towards the south-west. About ten o'clock we met a coffle of twenty-six people and seven loaded asses returning from the Gambia. Most of the men were armed with muskets, and had broad belts of scarlet cloth over their shoulders and European hats upon their heads. They informed us that there was very little demand for slaves on the coast, as no vessel had arrived for some months past. On hearing this the Serawoollies, who had travelled with us from the Falemé River, separated themselves and their slaves from the coffle. They had not, they said, the means of maintaining their slaves in Gambia until a vessel should arrive, and were unwilling to sell them to disadvantage; they therefore departed to the northward for Kajaaga. We continued our route through the wilderness, and travelled all day through a rugged country covered with extensive thickets of bamboo. At sunset, to our great joy, we arrived at a pool of water near a large tabba-tree, whence the place is called Tabbagee, and here we rested a few hours. The water at this season of the year is by no means plentiful in these woods, and as the days were insufferably hot Karfa proposed to travel in the night. Accordingly about eleven o'clock the slaves were taken out of their irons, and the people of the coffle received orders to keep close together, as well to prevent the slaves from attempting to escape as on account of the wild beasts. We travelled with great alacrity until daybreak, when it was discovered that a free woman had parted from the coffle in the night; her name was called until the woods resounded, but, no answer being given, we conjectured that she had either mistaken the road or that a lion had seized her unperceived. At length it was agreed that four people should go back a few miles to a small rivulet, where some of the coffle had stopped to drink as we passed it in the night, and that the coffle should wait for their return. The sun was about an hour high before the people came back with the woman, whom they found lying fast asleep by the stream. We now resumed our journey, and about eleven o'clock reached a walled town called Tambacunda, where we were well received. Here we remained four days on account of a palaver which was held on the following occasion:—Modi Lemina, one of the slatees belonging to the coffle, had formerly married a woman of this town, who had borne him two children; he afterwards went to Manding, and remained there eight years without sending any account of himself during all that time to his deserted wife, who, seeing no prospect of his return, at the end of three years had married another man, to whom she had likewise borne two children. Lemina now claimed his wife; but the second husband refused to deliver her up, insisting that by the laws of Africa when a man has been three years absent from his wife, without giving her notice of his being alive, the woman is at liberty to marry again. After all the circumstances had been fully investigated in an assembly of the chief men, it was determined that the wife should make her choice, and be at liberty either to return to the first husband, or continue with the second, as she alone should think proper. Favourable as this determination was to the lady, she found it a difficult matter to make up her mind, and requested time for consideration; but I think I could perceive that *first love* would carry the day. Lemina was indeed somewhat older than his rival, but he was also much richer. What weight this circumstance had in the scale of his wife's affections I pretend not to say.

On the morning of the 26th, as we departed from Tambacunda, Karfa observed to me that there were no shea-trees farther to the westward than this town. I had collected and brought with me from Manding the leaves and flowers of this tree, but they were so greatly bruised on the road that I thought it best to gather another specimen at this place. The appearance of the fruit evidently places the shea-tree in the natural order of *Sapotæ*, and it has some resemblance to the *mudhuca* tree described by Lieutenant Charles Hamilton in the "Asiatic Researches," vol. i., p. 300.

About one o'clock on the morning of the 26th we reached Sibikillin, a walled village; but the inhabitants having the character of inhospitality towards strangers, and of being much addicted to theft, we did not think proper to enter the gate. We rested a short time under a tree, and then continued our route until it was dark, when we halted for the night by a small stream running towards the Gambia. Next day the road led over a wild and rocky country, everywhere rising into hills and abounding with monkeys and wild beasts. In the rivulets among the hills we found great plenty of fish. This was a very hard day's journey; and it was not until sunset that we reached the village of Koomboo, near to which are the ruins of a large town formerly destroyed by war. The inhabitants of Koomboo, like those of Sibikillin, have so bad a reputation that strangers seldom lodge in the village; we accordingly rested for the night in the fields, where we erected temporary huts for our protection, there being great appearance of rain.

May 28.—We departed from Koomboo, and slept at a Foulah town, about seven miles to the westward; from which, on the day following, having crossed a considerable branch of the Gambia, called Neola Koba, we reached a well-inhabited part of the country. Here are several towns within sight of each other, collectively called Tenda, but each is distinguished also by its particular name. We lodged at one of them, called Koba Tenda, where we remained the day following, in order to procure provisions for our support in crossing the Simbani woods. On the 30th we reached Jallacotta, a considerable town, but much infested by Foulah banditti, who come through the woods from Bondou and steal everything they can lay their hands on. A few days before our arrival they had stolen twenty head of cattle, and on the day following made a second attempt, but were beaten off and one of them was taken prisoner. Here one of the slaves belonging to the coffle, who had travelled with great difficulty for the last three days, was found unable to proceed any farther: his master (a singing man) proposed therefore to exchange him for a young slave girl belonging to one of the townspeople. The poor girl was ignorant of her fate until the bundles were all tied up in the morning, and the coffle ready to depart, when, coming with some other young women to see the coffle set out, her master took her by the hand, and delivered her to the singing man. Never was a face of serenity more suddenly changed into one of the deepest distress; the terror she manifested on having the load put upon her head and the rope fastened round her neck, and the sorrow with which she bade adieu to her companions, were truly affecting. About nine o'clock we crossed a large plain covered with *ciboa*-trees (a species of palm), and came to the river Nerico, a branch of the Gambia. This was but a small river at this time, but in the rainy season it is often dangerous to travellers. As soon as we had crossed this river, the singing men began to vociferate a particular song, expressive of their joy at having got safe into the west country, or, as they expressed it, *the land of the setting sun*. The country was found to be very level, and the soil a mixture of clay and sand. In the afternoon it rained hard, and we had recourse to the common negro umbrella, a large ciboa-leaf, which, being placed upon the head, completely defends the whole body from the rain. We lodged for the night under the shade of a large tabba-tree, near the ruins of a village. On the morning following we crossed a stream called Noulico, and about two o'clock, to my infinite joy, I saw myself once more on the banks of the Gambia, which at this place, being deep and smooth, is navigable; but the people told me that a little lower down the stream is so shallow that the coffles frequently cross it on foot.

June 2.—We departed from Seesukunda and passed a number of villages, at none of which was the coffle permitted to stop, although we were all very much fatigued. It was four o'clock in the afternoon before we reached Baraconda, where we rested one day. Departing from Baraconda on the morning of the 4th, we reached in a few hours Medina, the capital of the king of Woolli's dominions, from whom the reader may recollect I received an hospitable reception in the beginning of December, 1795, in my journey eastward. I immediately inquired concerning the health of my good old benefactor, and learned with great concern that he was dangerously ill. As Karfa would not allow the coffle to stop, I could not present my respects to the king in person, but I sent him word by the officer to whom we paid customs that his prayers for my safety had not been unavailing. We continued our route until sunset, when we lodged at a small village a little to the westward of Kootacunda, and on the day following arrived at Jindey, where, eighteen months before, I had parted from my friend Dr. Laidley—an interval during which I had not beheld the face of a Christian, nor once heard the delightful sound of my native language.

Being now arrived within a short distance of Pisania, from whence my journey originally commenced, and learning that my friend Karfa was not likely to meet with an immediate opportunity of selling his slaves on the Gambia, it occurred to me to suggest to him that he would find it for his interest to leave them at Jindey until a market should offer. Karfa agreed with me in this opinion, and hired from the chief man of the town huts for their accommodation, and a piece of land on which to employ them in raising corn and other provisions for their maintenance. With regard to himself, he declared that he would not quit me until my departure from Africa. We set out accordingly—Karfa, myself, and one of the Foulahs belonging to the coffle—early on the morning of the 9th; but although I was now approaching the end of my tedious and toilsome journey, and expected in another day to meet with countrymen and friends, I could not part for the last time with my unfortunate fellow-travellers—doomed, as I knew most of them to be, to a life of captivity and slavery in a foreign land—without great emotion. During a wearisome peregrination of more than five hundred British miles, exposed to the burning rays of a tropical sun, these poor slaves, amidst their own infinitely greater sufferings, would commiserate mine, and, frequently of their own accord, bring water to quench my thirst, and at night collect branches and leaves to prepare me a bed in the wilderness. We parted with reciprocal expressions of regret and benediction. My good wishes and prayers were all I could bestow upon them, and it afforded me some consolation to be told that they were sensible I had no more to give.

My anxiety to get forward admitting of no delay on the road, we reached Tendacunda in the evening, and were hospitably received at the house of an aged black female called Seniora Camilla, a person who resided many years at the English factory and spoke our language. I was known to her before I had left the Gambia at the outset of my journey, but my dress and figure were now so different from the usual appearance of a European that she was very excusable in mistaking me for a Moor. When I told her my name and country she surveyed me with great astonishment, and seemed unwilling to give credit to the testimony of her senses. She assured me that none of the traders on the Gambia ever expected to see me again, having been informed long ago that the Moors of Ludamar had murdered me, as they had murdered Major Houghton. I inquired for my two attendants, Johnson and Demba, and learnt with great sorrow that neither of them was returned. Karfa, who had never before heard people converse in English, listened to us with great attention. Everything he saw seemed wonderful. The furniture of the house, the chairs, &c., and particularly beds with curtains, were objects of his great admiration, and he asked me a thousand questions concerning the utility and necessity of different articles, to some of which I found it difficult to give satisfactory answers.

On the morning of the 10th Mr. Robert Ainsley, having learned that I was at Tendacunda, came to meet me, and politely offered me the use of his horse. He informed me that Dr. Laidley had removed all his property to a place called Kayee, a little farther down the river, and that he was then gone to Doomasansa with his vessel to purchase rice, but would return in a day or two. He therefore invited me to stay with him at Pisania until the doctor's return. I accepted the invitation, and being accompanied by my friend Karfa, reached Pisania about ten o'clock. Mr. Ainsley's schooner was lying at anchor before the place. This was the most surprising object which Karfa had yet seen. He could not easily comprehend the use of the masts, sails, and rigging; nor did he conceive that it was possible, by any sort of contrivance, to make so large a body move forwards by the common force of the wind. The manner of fastening together the different planks which composed the vessel, and filling up the seams so as to exclude the water, was perfectly new to him; and I found that the schooner, with her cable and anchor, kept Karfa in deep meditation the greater part of the day.

About noon on the 12th Dr. Laidley returned from Doomasansa and received me with great joy and satisfaction, as one risen from the dead. Finding that the wearing apparel which I had left under his care was not sold or sent to England, I lost no time in resuming the English dress and disrobing my chin of its venerable encumbrance. Karfa surveyed me in my British apparel with great delight, but regretted exceedingly that I had taken off my beard, the loss of which, he said, had converted me from a man into a boy. Dr. Laidley readily undertook to discharge all the pecuniary engagements which I had entered into since my departure from the Gambia, and took my draft upon the association for the amount. My agreement with Karfa (as I have already related) was to pay him the value of one prime slave, for which I had given him my bill upon Dr. Laidley before we departed from Kamalia; for in case of my death on the road I was unwilling that my benefactor should be a loser. But this good creature had continued to manifest towards me so much kindness that I thought I made him but an inadequate recompense when I told him that he was now to receive double the sum I had originally promised; and Dr. Laidley assured him that he was ready to deliver the goods to that amount whenever he thought proper to send for them. Karfa was overpowered by this unexpected token of my gratitude, and still more so when he heard that I intended to send a handsome present to the good old schoolmaster, Fankooma, at Malacotta. He promised to carry up the goods along with his own; and Dr. Laidley assured him that he would exert himself in assisting him to dispose of his slaves to the best advantage the moment a slave vessel should arrive. These and other instances of attention and kindness shown him by Dr. Laidley were not lost upon Karfa. He would often say to me, "My journey has indeed been prosperous!" But observing the improved state of our manufactures and our manifest superiority in the arts of civilised life, he would sometimes appear pensive, and exclaim, with an involuntary sigh, *Fato fing inta feng* ("Black men are nothing")! At other times he would ask me, with great seriousness, what could possibly have induced me, who was no trader, to think of exploring so miserable a country as Africa. He meant by this to signify that, after what I must have witnessed in my own country, nothing in Africa could in his opinion deserve a moment's attention. I have preserved these little traits of character in this worthy negro, not only from regard to the man, but also because they appear to me to demonstrate that he possessed a mind *above his condition*. And to such of my readers as love to contemplate human nature in all its varieties, and to trace its progress from rudeness to refinement, I hope the account I have given of this poor African will not be unacceptable.

No European vessel had arrived at Gambia for many months previous to my return from the interior, and as the rainy season was now setting in I persuaded Karfa to return to his people at Jindey. He parted with me on the 14th with great tenderness; but as I had little hopes of being able to quit Africa for the remainder of the year, I told him, as the fact was, that I expected to see him again before my departure. In this, however, I was luckily disappointed, and my narrative now hastens to its conclusion; for on the 15th, the ship *Charlestown*, an American vessel, commanded by Mr. Charles Harris, entered the river. She came for slaves, intending to touch at Goree to fill up, and to proceed from thence to South Carolina. As the European merchants on the Gambia had at this time a great many slaves on hand, they agreed with the captain to purchase the whole of his cargo, consisting chiefly of rum and tobacco, and deliver him slaves to the amount in the course of two days. This afforded me such an opportunity of returning, though by a circuitous route, to my native country as I thought was not to be neglected. I therefore immediately engaged my passage in this vessel for America; and having taken leave of Dr. Laidley, to whose kindness I was so largely indebted, and my other friends on the river, I embarked at Kayee on the 17th day of June.

Our passage down the river was tedious and fatiguing; and the weather was so hot, moist, and unhealthy, that before our arrival at Goree four of the seamen, the surgeon, and three of the slaves had died of fevers. At Goree we were detained, for want of provisions, until the beginning of October.

The number of slaves received on board this vessel, both on the Gambia and at Goree, was one hundred and thirty, of whom about twenty-five had been, I suppose, of free condition in Africa, as most of those, being bushreens, could write a little Arabic. Nine of them had become captives in the religious war between Abdulkader and Damel, mentioned in the latter part of the preceding chapter. Two of the others had seen me as I passed through Bondou, and many of them had heard of me in the interior countries. My conversation with them, in their native language, gave them great comfort; and as the surgeon was dead I consented to act in a medical capacity in his room for the remainder of the voyage. They had in truth need of every consolation in my power to bestow; not that I observed any wanton acts of cruelty practised either by the master or the seamen towards them, but the mode of confining and securing negroes in the American slave-ships (owing chiefly to the weakness of their crews) being abundantly more rigid and severe than in British vessels employed in the same traffic, made these poor creatures to suffer greatly, and a general sickness prevailed amongst them. Besides the three who died on the Gambia, and six or eight while we remained at Goree, eleven perished at sea, and many of the survivors were reduced to a very weak and emaciated condition.

In the midst of these distresses the vessel, after having been three weeks at sea, became so extremely leaky as to require constant exertion at the pumps. It was found necessary therefore to take some of the ablest of the negro men out of irons and employ them in this labour, in which they were often worked beyond their strength. This produced a complication of miseries not easily to be described. We were, however, relieved much sooner than I expected, for, the leak continuing to gain upon us, notwithstanding our utmost exertions to clear the vessel, the seamen insisted on bearing away for the West Indies, as affording the only chance of saving our lives. Accordingly, after some objections on the part of the master, we directed our course for Antigua, and fortunately made that island in about thirty-five days after our departure from Goree. Yet even at this juncture we narrowly escaped destruction, for on approaching the north-west side of the island we struck on the Diamond Rock and got into St. John's Harbour with great difficulty. The vessel was afterwards condemned as unfit for sea, and the slaves, as I have heard, were ordered to be sold for the benefit of the owners.

At this island I remained ten days, when the *Chesterfield* packet, homeward bound from the Leeward Islands, touching at St. John's for the Antigua mail, I took my passage in that vessel. We sailed on the 24th of November, and after a short but tempestuous voyage arrived at Falmouth on the 22nd of December, from whence I immediately set out for London; having been absent from England two years and seven months.

NOTE.

The following passage from James Montgomery's poem, "The West Indies," published in 1810, was inspired by "Mungo Park's Travels in the Interior of Africa." It enshrines in English verse the beautiful incident of the negro woman's song of "Charity" (on page 190 of the first of these two volumes), and closes with the poet's blessing upon Mungo Park himself, who had sailed five years before upon the second journey, from which he had not returned, and whose fate did not become known until five years later.

Man, through all ages of revolving time,
Unchanging man, in every varying clime,
Deems his own land of every land the pride,
Beloved by Heaven o'er all the world beside;
His home the spot of earth supremely blest,
A dearer, sweeter spot than all the rest.
  And is the Negro outlawed from his birth?
Is he alone a stranger on the earth?
Is there no shed whose peeping roof appears
So lovely that it fills his eyes with tears?
No land, whose name, in exile heard, will dart
Ice through his veins and lightning through his heart?
Ah! yes; beneath the beams of brighter skies
His home amidst his father's country lies;
There with the partner of his soul he shares
Love-mingled pleasures, love-divided cares;
There, as with nature's warmest filial fire,
He soothes his blind and feeds his helpless sire;
His children, sporting round his hut, behold
How they shall cherish him when he is old,
Trained by example from their tenderest youth
To deeds of charity and words of truth.
Is *he* not blest? Behold, at closing day,
The Negro village swarms abroad to play;
He treads the dance, through all its rapturous rounds,
To the wild music of barbarian sounds;
Or, stretched at ease where broad palmettos shower
Delicious coolness in his shadowy bower,

He feasts on tales of witchcraft, that give birth
To breathless wonder or ecstatic mirth:
Yet most delighted when, in rudest rhymes,
The minstrel wakes the song of elder times,
When men were heroes, slaves to Beauty's charms,
And all the joys of life were love and arms.
Is not the Negro blest? His generous soil
With harvest plenty crowns his simple toil;
More than his wants his flocks and fields afford:
He loves to greet a stranger at his board:
"The winds were roaring and the White Man fled;
The rains of night descended on his head;
The poor White Man sat down beneath our tree:
Weary and faint and far from home was he:
For him no mother fills with milk the bowl,
No wife prepares the bread to cheer his soul.
Pity the poor White Man, who sought our tree;
No wife, no mother, and no home has he."
Thus sung the Negro's daughters;—once again,
O that the poor White Man might hear that strain!
Whether the victim of the treacherous Moor,
Or from the Negro's hospitable door
Spurned as a spy from Europe's hateful clime,
And left to perish for thy country's crime,
Or destined still, when all thy wanderings cease,
On Albion's lovely lap to rest in peace,
Pilgrim! in heaven or earth, where'er thou be,
Angels of mercy guide and comfort thee!

A note to the same poem gives the following record of facts, substantiated in a court of justice, in which there can be only one answer to the question, "Which were the savages?"

"In this year (1783) certain underwriters desired to be heard against Gregson and others of Liverpool, in the case of the ship *Zong*, Captain Collingwood, alleging that the captain and officers of the said vessel threw overboard one hundred and thirty-two slaves alive into the sea, in order to defraud them by claiming the value of the said slaves, as if they had been lost in a natural way. In the course of the trial which afterwards came on, it appeared that the slaves on board the *Zong* were very sickly; that sixty of them had already died, and several were ill and likely to die, when the captain proposed to James Kelsal, the mate, and others to throw several of them overboard, stating that 'if they died a natural death, the loss would fall upon the owners of the ship, but that if they were thrown into the sea, it would fall upon the underwriters.' He selected accordingly one hundred and thirty-two of the most sickly of the slaves. Fifty-four of these were immediately thrown overboard, and forty-two were made to be partakers of their fate on the succeeding day. In the course of three days afterwards the remaining twenty-six were brought upon deck to complete the number of victims. The first sixteen submitted to be thrown into the sea, but the rest, with a noble resolution, would not suffer the offices to touch them, but leaped after their companions and shared their fate.

"The plea which was set up in behalf of this atrocious and unparalleled act of wickedness was that the captain discovered, when he made the proposal, that he had only two hundred gallons of water on board, and that he had missed his port. It was proved, however, in answer to this, that no one had been put upon short allowance; and that, as if Providence had determined to afford an unequivocal proof of the guilt, a shower of rain fell, and continued for three days, immediately after the second lot of slaves had been destroyed, by means of which they might have filled many of their vessels with water, and thus have prevented all necessity for the destruction of the third.

"Mr. Granville Sharp (who after many years of struggle first obtained the decision of a court of justice that there *are* no slaves in England) was present at this trial, and procured the attendance of a shorthand writer to take down the facts which should come out in the course of it. These he gave to the public afterwards. He communicated them also, with a copy of the trial, to the Lords of the Admiralty, as the guardians of justice upon the seas, and to the Duke of Portland, as principal Minister of state. No notice, however, was taken by any of these of the information which had been thus sent them."

Another incident of the Middle Passage suggested to James Montgomery a poem called "The Voyage of the Blind."

> "It was that fatal and perfidious bark,
> Built in the eclipse, and rigged with curses dark."

Milton's Lycidas.

The ship *Le Rodeur*, Captain B., of 200 tons burthen, left Havre on the 24th of January, 1819, for the coast of Africa, and reached her destination on the 14th of March following, anchoring at Bonny, on the river Calabar. The crew, consisting of twenty-two men, enjoyed good health during the outward voyage and during their stay at Bonny, where they continued till the 6th of April. They had observed no trace of ophthalmia among the natives; and it was not until fifteen days after they had set sail on the return voyage, and the vessel was near the equator, that they perceived the first symptoms of this frightful malady. It was then remarked that the negroes, who to the number of 160 were crowded together in the hold and between the decks, had contracted a considerable redness of the eyes, which spread with singular rapidity. No great attention was at first paid to these symptoms, which were thought to be caused only by the want of air in the hold, and by the scarcity of water, which had already begun to be felt. At this time they were limited to eight ounces of water a day for each person, which quantity was afterwards reduced to the half of a wine-glass. By the advice of M. Maugnan, the surgeon of the ship, the negroes, who had hitherto remained shut up in the hold, were brought upon deck in succession, in order that they might breathe a purer air. But it became necessary to abandon this expedient, salutary as it was, because many of the negroes, affected with *nostalgia* (a passionate longing to return to their native land), threw themselves into the sea, locked in each other's arms.

The disease, which had spread itself so rapidly and frightfully among the Africans, soon began to infect all on board. The danger also was greatly increased by a malignant dysentery which prevailed at the time. The first of the crew who caught it was a sailor who slept under the deck near the grated hatch which communicated with the hold. The next day a landsman was seized with ophthalmia; and in three days more the captain and the whole ship's company, except one sailor, who remained at the helm, were blinded by the disorder.

All means of cure which the surgeon employed, while he was able to act, proved ineffectual. The sufferings of the crew, which were otherwise intense, were aggravated by apprehension of revolt among the negroes, and the dread of not being able to reach the West Indies, if the only sailor who had hitherto escaped the contagion, and on whom their whole hope rested, should lose his sight, like the rest. This calamity had actually befallen the *Leon*, a Spanish vessel which the *Rodeur* met on her passage, and the whole of whose crew, having become blind, were under the necessity of altogether abandoning the direction of their ship. These unhappy creatures, as they passed, earnestly entreated the charitable interference of the seamen of the *Rodeur*; but these, under their own affliction, could neither quit their vessel to go on board the

Leon, nor receive the crew of the latter into the *Rodeur*, where, on account of the cargo of negroes, there was scarcely room for themselves. The vessels therefore soon parted company, and the *Leon* was never seen nor heard of again, so far as could be traced at the publication of this narrative. In all probability, then, it was lost. On the fate of *this* vessel the poem is founded.

The *Rodeur* reached Guadaloupe on the 21st of June, 1819, her crew being in a most deplorable condition. Of the negroes, thirty-seven had become perfectly blind, twelve had lost each an eye, and fourteen remained otherwise blemished by the disease. Of the crew, twelve, including the surgeon, had entirely lost their sight; five escaped with an eye each, and four were partially injured.

FOOTNOTES.

[7] I should have before observed that I found the language of Bambarra a sort of corrupted Mandingo. After a little practice, I understood and spoke it without difficulty.

[35] There is another town of this name hereafter to be mentioned.

[58] From a plant called *kabba*, that climbs like a vine upon the trees.

[80] Soon after baptism the children are marked in different parts of the skin, in a manner resembling what is called *tattooing* in the South Sea Islands.

[82] Chap. xxxi. vv. 26–28.

[92] Poisoned arrows are used chiefly in war. The poison, which is said to be very deadly, is prepared from a shrub called *koono* (a species of *echites*), which is very common in the woods. The leaves of this shrub, when boiled with a small quantity of water, yield a thick black juice, into which the negroes dip a cotton thread: this thread they fasten round the iron of the arrow in such a manner that it is almost impossible to extract the arrow, when it has sunk beyond the barbs, without leaving the iron point and the poisoned thread in the wound.

[93] A minkalli is a quantity of gold nearly equal in value to ten shillings sterling.

[104] This is a large, spreading tree (a species of *sterculia*) under which the bentang is commonly placed.

[109] When a negro takes up goods on credit from any of the Europeans on the coast, and does not make payment at the time appointed, the European is authorised by the laws of the country to seize upon the debtor himself, if he can find him, or, if he cannot be found, on any person of his family; or, in

the last resort, on *any native of the same kingdom*. The person thus seized on is detained, while his friends are sent in quest of the debtor. When he is found, a meeting is called of the chief people of the place, and the debtor is compelled to ransom his friend by fulfilling his engagements. If he is unable to do this, his person is immediately secured and sent down to the coast, and the other released. If the debtor cannot be found, the person seized on is obliged to pay double the amount of the debt, or is himself sold into slavery. I was given to understand, however, that this part of the law is seldom enforced.

www.ingramcontent.com/pod-product-compliance
Lightning Source LLC
LaVergne TN
LVHW091200180726
843490LV00007B/2501